Graduate Study in the USA

This book is part of the Peter Lang Education list.
Every volume is peer reviewed and meets
the highest quality standards for content and production.

PETER LANG
New York • Bern • Frankfurt • Berlin
Brussels • Vienna • Oxford • Warsaw

Graduate Study in the USA

Surviving and Succeeding

Christopher McMaster & Caterina Murphy, Editors

PETER LANG
New York • Bern • Frankfurt • Berlin
Brussels • Vienna • Oxford • Warsaw

Library of Congress Cataloging-in-Publication Data

Names: McMaster, Christopher (Christopher Todd), editor. |
Murphy, Caterina, editor.
Title: Graduate study in the USA: surviving and succeeding /
edited by Christopher McMaster, Caterina Murphy.
Other titles: Graduate study in the United States of America
Description: New York: Peter Lang, 2016. | Includes bibliographical references.
Identifiers: LCCN 2015038802| ISBN 9781433129902 (hardcover: alk. paper) |
ISBN 9781433129896 (paperback: alk. paper) | ISBN 9781453915370 (e-book)
Subjects: LCSH: Universities and colleges—United States—
Graduate work—Handbooks, manuals, etc. | Graduate students—
United States—Handbooks, manuals, etc.
Classification: LCC LB2371.4.G729 2016 | DDC 378.1/55—dc23
LC record available at http://lccn.loc.gov/2015038802

Bibliographic information published by **Die Deutsche Nationalbibliothek**.
Die Deutsche Nationalbibliothek lists this publication in the "Deutsche
Nationalbibliografie"; detailed bibliographic data are available
on the Internet at http://dnb.d-nb.de/.

Cover art by Tara Murphy
Cover design by Clear Point Designs

The paper in this book meets the guidelines for permanence and durability
of the Committee on Production Guidelines for Book Longevity
of the Council of Library Resources.

© 2016 Peter Lang Publishing, Inc., New York
29 Broadway, 18th floor, New York, NY 10006
www.peterlang.com

Printed in the United States of America

Contents

Foreword

Surviving the Rat Race and Becoming Citizen Professionals

HARRY C. BOYTE

As the subtitle (*Surviving and Succeeding*) suggests, *Graduate Study in the USA* is a survival kit for troubled times.

The collection could hardly come at a better time. Against a backdrop of mounting college debt and uncertain job prospects for many college graduates, a chorus of observers has described what Lindsey Cook (2014) in *US News & World Report* called the "frenzy" associated with college. "It's not a pretty picture in the ecology overall" said Mitchell Stevens (Cook, 2014), who recently published *Creating a Class: College Admissions and the Education of Elites.*

> It's a hyper competitiveness for a small number of schools and a mal-distribution of seats in the more open access. There are 5,000 colleges and universities in the United States; there are plenty of seats in the system overall. There are just a limited number of seats at the top. (Cook, 2014)

Such pressures lead to growing anxiety and depression. According to UCLA's American Freshman Survey, which surveys more than 150,000 first-year freshmen each year, students' emotional health dropped to an all-time low in 2014 (Bidwell, 2015). Graduate students also show the strains of today's hypercompetitive achievement culture. Writing in *Science,* Carrie Arnold (2014) analyzed recent studies and found that almost 60% of grad students reported feeling overwhelmed, exhausted, hopeless, sad, or depressed nearly all the time. One in 10 said they had thought about suicide in the past year. Tammy Wyatt and Sara Oswalt analyzed responses from graduate students surveyed by the American College Health Association and found that 78.5% said they felt overwhelmed in the past year and 54.5% said they had felt stress ranging from "more than average" to "tremendous" (Arnold, 2014).

Individual stories convey the subtle pressures in graduate education to conform and compete. Jamie Haft (2015), writing in *Democracy's Education,* a collection of strategies and stories to revitalize the public purposes of higher education, quoted one fellow student in the Tisch School of Arts at New York University who told her, "I put this pressure on myself when I'm at school to reject my community and home." Another said, "Everyone thinks identity is an individual thing, and if you're not blazing your own path, tearing down traditions and creating something new, then it's not worthwhile" (p. 143). In a similar vein, Cecilia Orphan (2015), a graduate student in education at the University of Pennsylvania, reported from conversations with her colleagues in grad school across the country that "doctoral students feel that they must adjust or sacrifice their own interests and goals (often the very interests and questions that led them to graduate school) to fit the expectations and interests of their advisors" (p. 149).

Graduate Study in the USA, full of tips and tools drawn from real-world graduate student experiences and expressed in many voices, addresses these pressures, tensions, and stresses. A sample of the titles suggests the range: "Making the Most of the Conference Experience," "How to Turn a Good Relationship with Your Supervisor into a Great One," "We're Not in the Barrio Anymore: Negotiating Chicana/o Guilt in the Ivory Tower," "Navigating Academia's Invisible Margins: *Different* (dis)Abilities in Graduate Studies," and "Navigating Academic Culture Shock: Advice for International Students" as some examples.

The book is, also, not simply about survival.

In the practices taught by community organizing, a foundational concept is the need to hold in balance "the world as it is" and "the world as it should be," the world as one would like it to be. The world as it is begins with a realistic assessment of different interests, viewpoints, norms, values, and power relationships. Those interested in making change often live in the world as it "should be," as they want it to be. Yet without realism, effective action to make change is very unlikely. This can be called "citizen politics," beyond the politics of ideology owned by detached politicians. Citizen politics is owned by citizens who develop practical skills of working on problems in their everyday lives and environments and who develop in the process the capacity to make larger changes.

A great strength of *Graduate Study in the USA* is the real-world, practical, clear-eyed quality of virtually all the chapters. The contributors don't whine, moan, or complain. With vivid stories and clear expository writing they advance ideas and strategies for what has worked for them and what they believe might work for others.

The aim is not simply survival but also success and well-being, the theme of Part 4 ("Maintaining Wellness: Looking After You"). Nicholas Werse and B. J. Parker's chapter is titled, "The Student's Practical Guide to Not Losing Your Soul." Tabatha Hoffmeyer writes about "Finding Inspiration in Grad School." Rebecca Zimmer's chapter is "Seeing the Stars."

In Part 2, "The Flourishing Academic," Christopher McMaster, one of the editors, talks about the wise advice he once received from a younger colleague to "think bigger." This book is one result of doing exactly that.

This is not simply a book about accepting the world as it is. Both the survival strategies and the hopes for flourishing challenge the individualist bent of today's high-stakes graduate education with more community-oriented values and cooperative practices. Debra Trusty's chapter calls for a move beyond the go-it-alone tendency of graduate norms. She gives a step-by-step blueprint for "Starting and Managing a Dissertation Support Group." Raisa Alvarado Uchima and Jaime Guzmán stress the importance of maintaining contact with home cultural communities. Danielle Shepherd argues for "Engaging the Next Generation of Professional Students." And the whole collection in its design and authorship disrupts singular notions of "who" graduate students are supposed to be, or "how" they are supposed to know and act.

Overall these students point beyond what Parker Palmer (1993) called the "objectivist" approach to knowledge, which separates the knower from the object to be known. This separation, wrote Palmer,

> holds us at arm's length as detached analysts, commentators, evaluators of each other and the world. Like theater-goers, we are free to watch, applaud, hiss and boo, but we do not understand ourselves as an integral part of the action. (p. 23)

As Palmer (1993) has discovered and communicated through decades of work in higher education, objectivist separation, another name for a culture of detachment, works enormous anguish for many scholars.

I saw this firsthand in 1997 when the Kellogg Foundation asked the Center for Democracy and Citizenship (which I had initiated at the University of Minnesota's Humphrey Institute of Public Affairs a decade before), to assess whether the public service mission of the university could be revived. We knew from Cornell professor Scott Peters's research that the university had once had a rich history of reciprocal involvement, public work with the state through faculty and student research and engagement as part of its "land grant mission."

When chair of the Political Science Department Edwin Fogelman and I interviewed dozens of senior faculty, many at the UMN for decades, we heard again and again how much such connectedness had weakened. We often heard, as well, feelings of anguish about the process voiced by faculty who had never communicated their views to other colleagues. Studies such as *American Academic Culture in*

Transformation, edited by Thomas Bender and Karl Schorske (1998), help explain some of what's been going on. Bender and Schorske showed how academic incentive structures weaken the "compact" between higher education and society.[1]

Changing ideas of research, especially in the sciences, have also had an impact, feeding into what can be called a technocratic paradigm of one-way dispensing of knowledge by outside experts. Scientists—and, more broadly, scientifically trained disciplinary professionals of all kinds—have come to view civic life and other citizens from the outside. "The scientists who powerfully shaped the national discourse on science in the middle years of the twentieth century drew a sharp line between science and society," wrote Harvard historian Andrew Jewett (2011) in his recent study, *Science, Democracy, and the American University.* "They portrayed science as utterly deaf to human concerns." Jewett argued that this view reversed a once robust movement of "scientific democrats" who saw science not as "value free" but rather as practices and values such as cooperative inquiry and testing of ideas in real life, which all citizens of a democratic society needed to learn (p. 310).

The prevailing culture of detachment results in the individualist, hypercompetitive, meritocratic values that create stress among bright and talented graduate students. It has to change for the sake of students, higher education, and the society. Moreover, there is strong evidence that graduate students and young faculty *want* the culture of detachment to change. As Timothy Eatman (2015) has found in a study of more than 500 young faculty and graduate students, for young scholars "the arc of academic career bends toward publicly engaged scholarship." In his essay in the *Democracy's Education* collection, Eatman quoted a collective letter to the editor of the *Chronicle of Higher Education,* responding to "Syracuse's Slide," a front-page *Chronicle* article that noted a drop in *US News & World Report* rankings. The article had voiced the views of a small group of disgruntled faculty that Syracuse University was becoming too committed to community engagement and inclusive admission. Nancy Cantor, the chancellor, sought to revitalize the "democracy's college" tradition of public universities, land grant colleges, HBCUs and City College of New York. City College, which admitted all high school students in New York desiring to attend and gave a free education, was dedicated to a concept of cooperative excellence—that a mix of students and faculty from diverse backgrounds, interacting in a highly stimulating environment of high public expectation and purpose, could achieve greatness that a focus on winnowing out the individual stars could never achieve. The students' letter, in the vein of this democracy tradition, read

> We write to share our stories of engaged research, teaching, learning, and civic life as citizens of Syracuse, N.Y., and students of the university. Far from experiencing or perceiving a decrease in the rigor of our educational experience, we acknowledge what a privilege

it is to grow in our disciplines through sharing and co-creating knowledge with diverse and valuable communities… [we want] to speak back and express our belief that engaged scholarship powerfully adds to our academic experience, combats the out-of-date "Ivory Tower" metaphor, and rigorously contributes to our academic community. (Eatman, 2015, pp. 132–133)

This letter summarizes the widespread sentiments of a fledgling movement of graduate students and others in higher education who aspire to be "citizen professionals," contributing to the democratic purposes of higher education. Citizen professionals and citizen scholars, far more than narrow disciplinary experts in conversation only with others in their disciplines, are professionals who see themselves as "part of" the life of communities and society, not "instructors of" or even "partners with."

The contributors to *Graduate Study in the USA* are most certainly developing as citizen scholars and citizen professionals who aspire to be part of the democracy.

NOTE

1. For a summary of the faculty reviews see Harry Boyte's (2000) *Public Engagement in a Civic Mission*.

REFERENCES

Arnold, C. (2014, February 04). Paying graduate school's mental toll. *Science*. Retrieved from http://sciencecareers.sciencemag.org/career_magazine/previous_issues/articles/2014_02_04/caredit.a1400031

Bender, T., & Schorske, K. (1998). *American academic cultures in transformation: Fifty years, four disciplines*. Princeton, NJ: Princeton University Press.

Bidwell, A. (2015, February 6). College freshmen socialize less, feel depressed more. *US News & World Report*. Retrieved from http://www.usnews.com/news/blogs/data-mine/2015/02/06/college-freshmen-socialize-less-feel-depressed-more

Boyte, H. (2000). *Public engagement in a civic mission*. Dayton, OH: Kettering Foundation. Retrieved from https://www.kettering.org/sites/default/files/product-downloads/Public_Engagement.pdf

Cook, L. (2014, September 22). Is the college admissions bubble about to burst? *US News & World Report*. Retrieved from http://www.usnews.com/news/blogs/data-mine/2014/09/22/is-the-college-admissions-bubble-about-to-burst

Eatman, T. (2015). The emerging citizenry of academe. In H. C. Boyte (Ed.), *Democracy's education: Public work, citizenship, and the future of colleges and universities* (pp. 131–138). Nashville, TN: Vanderbilt University Press.

Haft, J. (2015). Becoming a civic artist. In H. C. Boyte (Ed.), *Democracy's education: Public work, citizenship, and the future of colleges and universities* (pp. 141–146). Nashville, TN: Vanderbilt University Press.

Jewett, A. (2011). *Science, democracy, and the American university: From the civil war to the cold war.* Cambridge, MA: Harvard University Press.

Orphan, C. (2015). What's doctoral education got to do with it? In H. C. Boyte (Ed.), *Democracy's education: Public work, citizenship, and the future of colleges and universities* (pp. 147–153). Nashville, TN: Vanderbilt University Press.

Palmer, P. (1993). *To know as we are known.* New York, NY: HarperCollins.

Preface and Acknowledgments

CHRISTOPHER MCMASTER AND CATERINA MURPHY

Graduate Study in the USA: Surviving and Succeeding is the second *Surviving and Succeeding* book to be published by us and is part of a global series currently in production. It reflects the issues and concerns of graduate students in the USA. It is written by students in the United States, those currently working on their graduate degree in a USA institution, or recent graduates. We feel a sense of surety in knowing that the voices within the book, the stories of the graduate students and graduates and the vulnerabilities they often expose, do reflect what it takes to survive and succeed while undertaking graduate study in the USA.

Before writing each chapter the contributors were given this simple instruction by the editors:

> If you could go back in time to when you started your graduate studies, what would you tell your younger/less-experienced self? What advice could you give to prospective or current graduate students now, with the wisdom of your hindsight?

Each chapter is written with this in mind, and prioritises the relationship between writer and reader.

This book can be read cover to cover, or it can be treated like a guide book to a city you have not visited before, where you dip in and out of sections or chapters that are especially pertinent to you at the time. The point of the book is to show what is on offer, what may be expected, how to prepare for the unexpected, and how to make your travels through graduate study in the USA a rewarding experience.

The book is divided into five parts, each covering key elements for surviving and succeeding in graduate study. The first part examines the mechanics of graduate study and covers essentials such as advisory relationships, scholarships, conferencing, and building support networks. The second part concentrates on succeeding as an academic and includes writing, editing, and publishing, as well as the responsibility of being an academic. The third part considers understanding and navigating difference in academia. Part 4 focuses on maintaining health, well-being, and balance when working for long, concentrated periods of study, and the final section is about studying from and in another culture, whether that be an American abroad, or a student new to America.

Note: while the editors appreciate and accept the significant contribution of each chapter to the book as a whole, they do not necessarily endorse all viewpoints expressed within them.

We wish to pay tribute to:

- All the contributing authors, without whom this book would not have eventuated—thank you to you all;
- The staff at Peter Lang for their extremely professional work in bringing this book to print;
- The many graduate associations that forwarded the call for abstracts to their many members, and those bloggers that similarly passed on the word, and Paula Cambers at Versatile PhD (https://versatilephd.com/) for helping to get the call out.
- Dr. Aubrey Threlkeld for his support in the early stages of developing this book.
- My (Caterina's) husband Anthony, for his support, patience, and encouragement in getting this next book in our global series completed.

Cover art:

Tara Murphy is a young New Zealand artist living and working in Auckland who creates original sculpture for commissions, solo and group exhibitions and national art awards. She also teaches after school art classes for young children.

Her work utilizes found 'natural' wood and processed timber off-cuts. Transforming wood that is essentially 'firewood' into sculpture, holds a re-occurring significance in the overall themes that her work explores. Revelling in the simplicity of the hand-made, Tara enjoys the slow, methodical work that comes with using hand tools and making her own natural stains, polishes and solutions.

Her work is commissioned to overseas and New Zealand clients. She can be contacted at www.taramurphy.me

PART ONE

Basic Mechanics
of Graduate Study

CHAPTER ONE

Making the Most of the Conference Experience

MELISSA DENNIHY

INTRODUCTION

When I was a graduate student, I often wondered if presenting at conferences would be a misuse of time—I worried that few people would come to a talk by a graduate student, and that I would merely read my paper to a small audience and fly home, feeling that I could have spent my weekend more productively by working on my dissertation or grading student papers. But since I had heard repeatedly that conference participation is crucial for graduate students, I felt compelled to attend conferences. To avoid misusing time that could've been spent more productively, I learned to make the most of the conference experience by capitalizing on the many opportunities conferences offer.

While attending conferences is an important part of the successful graduate student's career, if conferences are not selected carefully and time at a conference is not spent wisely conferencing *can* be a misuse of time for a student with a busy schedule and tight budget. However, making the most of the conference experience offers a wealth of opportunities for a graduate student seeking to network, publish, and prepare for an academic career.

This chapter discusses the key aspects of successful conferencing: how to choose conferences, write abstracts, find travel funding, and successfully present a paper. It also offers advice on what to do at conferences, *aside* from presenting, including how to network and seek out professionalization opportunities. In addition, I'll discuss important steps to take post-conference in order to stay in touch with new contacts and pursue further opportunities for your research. Given the many responsibilities graduate students juggle—coursework, exams, research, publishing, and teaching—this chapter suggests when, why, and how conferencing can be a productive step toward a successful career.

SELECTING CONFERENCES

Once you are enrolled in a graduate program, you will find that conference calls for papers (CFPs) are everywhere around you: posted on department bulletin boards, announced by professors and fellow students, and circulated on your program's listserv. It can be tempting to apply to any conference that seems interesting (or even to choose a conference because of its desirable location). However, it is important to consider the scholarly persona you are trying to cultivate and the long-term research agenda you plan to establish.

Graduate students who might start out taking classes on a range of topics are soon expected to specialize in order to write their dissertations and find jobs in a market where positions are becoming increasingly specific (in my field of English, for example, one will not find job posts seeking someone with a PhD in English, but posts for positions in specialized sub-areas of the field as diverse as Shakespearean studies, Latino literatures, and graphic genres). When I started out as a graduate student in English, I submitted abstracts to conferences focused on literatures from a myriad of times and places—my first three conference presentations were on 18th-century Irish literature, 20th-century African literature, and post-9/11 American literature. I saw nothing wrong with this; after all, I had taken a variety of courses and had seminar papers on all sorts of topics, so why not present as many of these papers as possible? However, at one point after I had gone to several conferences, an advisor reviewing my CV asked which of these areas I was actually interested in—I had presented on such a haphazard array of topics that she had no sense of what my research interests really were.

As you choose conferences to apply to, consider which of your work matters most to you, and which work you can envision becoming dissertation material. Looking even further into the future, consider that when you are applying for jobs, someone reviewing your CV should be able to see the continuities and connections among your presentations to get a sense of what your research has focused on over the past few years. Don't apply to any and every conference, but choose conferences that align with the research interests you are beginning to develop.

Choosing regional and national conferences that are larger and more prestigious is also a smart decision, as these are likely to be well worth your time. It's fine to present at graduate student conferences before starting your dissertation, and especially when you are new to conferencing. These smaller forums provide a more relaxed and less intimidating environment to get practice at presenting your work. But once you have started your dissertation and are thinking about entering the job market, it is important to begin presenting your work at large-scale regional and national conferences alongside other scholars in your discipline. If you only have time and money to go to one conference a year, apply to a conference held by a major organization in your field (in English, for example, the most important annual conference is held by the Modern Language Association; anthropologists attend the annual meeting of the American Anthropological Association, etc.). Presentations at these conferences will have the most value once you are on the job market, and will facilitate far more contacts with scholars in your field than attending graduate student conferences. Major conferences also give you a sense of the wider scholarly conversations occurring, knowledge that is useful in seeking to make your own work relevant and publishable.

SUBMITTING AN ABSTRACT

Because they are important events for academics at any level, regional and national conferences are quite competitive, and getting accepted requires that you write a strong abstract. An abstract is a clear and succinct proposal, usually between 250 and 500 words, explaining what you will address in your conference presentation. Your first step in writing a successful abstract is to re-read the conference CFP, or, in the case of conferences that do not accept individual submissions, to search the panel proposals and their CFPs. Determine the major themes and topics, and demonstrate in your abstract how and why your paper is a good fit. Your abstract should also make clear that you actually have an argument to present. As obvious as this may seem, a surprising number of abstracts merely *summarize* an issue, problem, or topic without explaining what the author's unique contribution, insight, or intervention is. Be sure your abstract clearly states what is original or significant about your work. Finally, make certain that the scope of your proposed talk is appropriate for a conference. A conference presentation generally lasts 15 to 20 minutes, which, if you read from a double-spaced typed paper, translates to 7 to 10 pages of material. As such, the scope of a conference paper is necessarily different from that of the 20–30 page seminar paper. If you submit an abstract that is too far-reaching in its scope, proposing to cover more than could likely be addressed in a conference presentation, panel organizers will worry about your ability to present effectively in the time available. This is also why following the CFP's word limit is important—if you can't write an abstract that respects the word count requested, you may raise concerns about whether you'll be able to give your talk in the time allotted.

PANEL PRESENTATIONS

If you are just starting a research project and are not yet ready to present a paper, you might propose a panel related to your research in which you act as chairperson without presenting. Reviewing abstracts submitted to your panel lets you encounter a range of ideas, texts, and approaches related to your research, and the panel itself will enable you to hear talks you have selected as particularly interesting and relevant to your own interests. Organizing and chairing a panel can thus be as beneficial to the earlier stages of research as presenting on panels is in later stages of one's research. Acting as panel chairperson also puts you in a leadership role at the conference, as chairs often organize post-panel dinners or drinks, which are useful opportunities for networking. However, be aware that chairing a panel is not always viewed as equivalent to presenting on one; in some cases, funding for conferences is only available for those presenting a paper.

FINANCIAL CONSIDERATIONS

Conferences can present serious financial challenges to graduate students; in addition to requiring a good chunk of time, travel, and hotel accommodation, not to mention registration fees, meals, and other smaller expenses, can easily add up to several hundred dollars or more. However, conference costs can often be fully or partially covered by funding from internal and external sources. After you receive confirmation that your conference proposal has been accepted, seek funding from your program and institution (the availability of such funds is something you should inquire about as a prospective graduate student). You can also seek funding from the conference organizers or sponsoring association, which may offer graduate student travel grants. Some organizations also offer travel support to contingent faculty, which any graduate student employed as an adjunct instructor qualifies for. If you are living off a graduate student salary and do not have much income to spare, you should not spend a substantial amount of your own money to attend a conference, unless you are on the job market and are attending the conference for interviews. If your funding options are limited, look for conferences in your area, or close enough that you could attend without flying or staying overnight. Major organizations usually list future conference locations several years in advance, so you could also check whether a conference being held across the country this year might take place in a nearby city next year. If you do secure funding, keep copies of your receipts as you travel, as you'll need these for reimbursement. This may seem obvious, but the stress of traveling and presenting might push the obvious out of your mind when you are on your trip. Post a note somewhere that will be easily visible when you're on the go such as on the handle of your suitcase.

PREPARING FOR THE CONFERENCE

You've applied to a conference that fits your research interests, received an acceptance notification, and secured funding. Now you need to prepare the presentation itself. There are a few points to bear in mind as you do this.

First, although most conference presenters do read from papers (or, increasingly, laptops), the best presenters make their presentations feel more like talks. Nobody likes to listen to someone read off a page, so as you prepare your presentation, think about delivery: build in notes or spacing that cue you to pause, look up, address your audience, and make eye contact. You can also try looking over each page of your paper until you are able to talk through the points on it without needing to continuously glance back at it or read straight through it.

You should also remember that a conference presentation is not a seminar paper. Focus on delivering your own ideas, particularly those that pack the greatest punch, and scale back on lengthy literature reviews or re-hashings of other arguments. If you are developing your talk by condensing a seminar paper, you may be frustrated by how much material you have to leave out (not just literature reviews, but your own ideas as well). Instead of trying to squeeze too much in to one talk, consider how parts of the paper you can't fit into this presentation might become material for future conference talks. Highlight these sections or save them as separate documents, and come back to them later.

When your paper is 7 to 10 pages long practice reading it aloud and timing yourself. It may take longer than expected to get through the material, and it is crucial that you can finish your talk in the time allotted. Using more time than you've been granted is unprofessional, and you don't want to put the panel chairperson in the uncomfortable position of having to cut you off before you've finished. It is also terribly ineffective to have to rush through your material because you've included too much. If, in practicing your paper, you go over your time limit, even by as little as one or two minutes, make the necessary revisions and avoid added stress during your presentation.

Practice Runs

Since it's important to practice delivering your paper, you might arrange a mock conference presentation beforehand. Your program may hold mock conference sessions, or you can organize your own mock talk and invite fellow students, mentors, and advisors. Even a parent or spouse who might not understand the talk's content can offer advice on things such as the pacing and volume of your speech and how engaging you are. It is easy to tell yourself not to be nervous about presenting, but it is much harder to put this advice into practice. The more time you spend presenting your material to audiences before the conference, however small or informal, the easier it will be to present on your big day.

Dress to Impress

One other thing to prepare before the conference is your attire. It is important to dress professionally: as someone new to the conference experience looking to establish a reputation and make connections, you want to look your best. Dressing professionally will also make you *feel* more professional, and this is one of the more useful aspects of conferencing: getting practice at performing a professional persona that commands the attention and respect of others.

GIVING YOUR PRESENTATION

No matter how many times you've practiced your talk, when you present you may move through the material more quickly or slowly than you intended to. Remain conscious of your pacing. Although the panel chairperson will likely inform you when your time is running out, you may want to keep time yourself by locating the room's clock or casually glancing at your watch. You don't want to be surprised by the chairperson flashing you a 2-minute warning when you still have four pages to read.

In addition to giving your own presentation, it's important to remember that when you present at a conference in the USA you are usually part of a panel. Be sure not to tune out when other panelists present. Especially if it's your first time presenting, you may be so nervous before your own talk, and so relieved afterward, that you fail to listen to your fellow panelists. However, questions from the audience and chairperson will often ask panelists to discuss their work in relation to the other presentations. It doesn't look collegial if you can't find anything to say about your co-panelists' presentations, so listen and jot down notes as they present.

You should also use the panel as an opportunity to network with fellow panelists. As I discuss further in the next section, conferences are as much about networking as presenting. Get to your panel early, and use the time to chat with fellow panelists about who they are and what they do. This can lead to fruitful connections and opportunities: another panelist might be putting together a book collection related to the panel topic, or serve on the editorial board of a journal in need of readers. In one way or another, the people you present alongside will likely have interests similar to yours and be involved in things that may be of interest to you. Learning about what others do, and how you might become involved in such opportunities, is exactly how networking works. Let's turn, then, to a discussion of the networking and professionalization opportunities conferences offer, and what to do with your time when you aren't presenting.

NETWORKING AND PROFESSIONALIZATION OPPORTUNITIES

Your conference presentation is a mere 20 minutes, but conferences are often 3 or 4 days. What should you do with the rest of your time? National conferences, especially, can be intimating, but resist the temptation to hide in a coffee shop or head straight back to your hotel room after your presentation. Instead, use this as an opportunity to practice developing your scholarly persona. Whether or not you're a student, you are there as an academic. Act as such: don't sit silently in the back of the room at every panel; mingle with people before and after panels, and ask questions during them.

Choosing which panels to attend can be difficult. At a larger conference, there will be dozens of panels each day, many happening simultaneously. Use your time to attend the panels most relevant to your research and career goals. Start by scanning the conference program for panels related to your research. These panels can inform you of relevant scholarship you may need to read, and make you aware of how to differentiate your project from related work others are doing. Many conferences also offer panels on publishing, teaching undergraduate classes, and succeeding on the academic job market. Go to these panels, listen carefully, ask questions, and take copious notes. These are unique opportunities to receive career advice from scholars besides your own mentors. There may also be "Meet the Editor" sessions where you can talk to editors of journals and presses. Check the program for these sessions, and make them a top priority when making your conference schedule. They are invaluable for learning about the types of work different journals and presses publish, and how your work may or may not be a good fit for certain venues.

In addition to going to relevant panels, take time to visit press displays. Another reason major conferences are more worthwhile than graduate student conferences is because they attract a far larger number of presses, which means increased opportunities to look at the books defining your field and meet the editors who are publishing them. Simply walking around a display and observing the books—including which ones are propped up and which lie in stacks underneath—can prove informative in terms of learning the types of work different presses publish and showcase. You also don't need to have a book proposal or project to talk to editors and learn about which presses might, down the line, be the best fit for the type of work you do. If editors are free when you visit a press display, you can ask them about their press's vision, what titles have been particularly successful in recent years, and what topics the press is most interested in pursuing in the future. Hanging around press displays can also provide opportunities to "overhear" conversations between editors and more senior scholars as the latter attempt to propose a book or secure a contract. Learning how to successfully talk about your research and why it matters—in other words, how to pitch and promote your work—is a difficult skill that most graduate students receive minimal training in. It's never too early to start working on this skill, and listening to scholars pitch their work to editors can be an enormously valuable learning experience.

You can also use conferences to learn about sub-organizations of interest to you. Regional and national academic associations are often made up of smaller organizations or committees that address the more specialized interests of different scholars. These organizations usually have their own membership meetings at the national annual conference, as well as their own panels. Connecting with a sub-organization that meets your interests more closely can help you feel less alienated and adrift at a large conference, and makes it easier to network with the people whose work most closely relates to yours. Becoming involved with a sub-organization can also lead to further opportunities in the future—for example, you might learn about opportunities to help organize future panels or to serve on the sub-organization's executive committee. Such service to the profession is impressive and valuable for a graduate student, and an excellent way to form relationships with scholars in your field beyond your home institution.

After a long day of panels and networking, it may be tempting to curl up in your hotel bed and sleep (or spend some time tackling that dissertation chapter or stack of student papers you brought along on the trip). However, try your best to be social and continue networking after each day's sessions are over. Sometimes, the most meaningful connections made at a conference are formed over dinner or drinks, rather than during a panel. Make it a point to reach out to panelists and other people you meet about dinner plans or activities around the city, and certainly accept any invitations for dinner or drinks extended to you. Many conferences also organize group outings you can sign up for: tours of the city's historical and cultural sites, tickets to plays, etc. These are useful opportunities to meet and connect with conference-goers aside from your fellow panelists.

AFTER THE CONFERENCE

When you get home from a conference, type up notes from panels right away, while they are still fresh in your memory. Another thing to do right away is add your presentation to your CV. If you don't do this immediately, you may forget about it, particularly as you start to go to more and more conferences. Having regional and national conference presentations on your CV is undoubtedly a way of making yourself stand out on the job market, so don't make the mistake of leaving out any talks you've given over the years.

You can also reach out to new contacts shortly after returning from the conference. Send e-mails to fellow panelists, editors, and other new acquaintances expressing that it was nice to meet them. Thank panel chairpersons for organizing the panel. Follow up on any opportunities others may have offered ("we talked at the conference about my reviewing that new book for your journal—I'd love to do that").

Perhaps the most important thing to do after a conference is continue developing the material you presented. A conference paper is often the start to a publication, and feedback from co-panelists and audience members, combined with the post-conference buzz, can provide excellent motivation to keep you writing and revising in the weeks afterward. If you let the paper lapse, you may never return to it, but if you push yourself to develop the presentation into a full article you might have a potential publication ready in a few months' time.

Finally, if you find a particular conference to be enjoyable and worthwhile, go again. There are a number of advantages to sticking with the same conference(s), rather than attending a different conference each year. Attending the same conference annually makes networking easier, as you start to recognize familiar faces and build relationships. Having a long-term affiliation with an organization also makes your scholarship and professional reputation seem more stable—floating from one conference to the next might suggest you can't find the right audience for your work or commit to the same set of research interests. Finding the right conference can provide a professional "home away from home," turning an experience that was once nerve-wracking into something to look forward to each year.

CONCLUSION

Successful conferencing can make a number of positive contributions to a graduate student's developing career it can facilitate contacts and connections, lead to future publications, and provide myriad forms of professional development.

Though conferences must be selected carefully, and time at conferences must be used wisely, if conferencing is approached in the right way the experience offers a wide range of useful and important opportunities for those beginning careers in academia.

CHAPTER TWO

Give Yourself a Chance

Apply for a Scholarship

MAGDALENA LESZKO

INTRODUCTION

The graduate schools in the United States are well known for their professional opportunities and prestige, but they can also be costly. Therefore, before
or during your graduate career you might consider applying for scholarships,
which provide a great opportunity to share research ideas and build a network
with other researchers. In addition, they enhance professional skills and provide
financial security. This chapter draws on my experience of successfully applying
for a Fulbright scholarship and later becoming a member of a scholarship review
committee. I applied for a scholarship to study in the United States shortly
before finishing my master's thesis in Psychology in Poland. Upon receiving the
funds, I did not have to worry about the cost of tuition or living expenses for the
entire year.

   During my graduate studies I continued applying for various scholarships and
I learned the key points that make a strong application. In this chapter I share
suggestions on how to effectively go through the rigorous process of applying for
a scholarship. This chapter will provide a brief overview of application procedures
and demonstrate a few effective strategies that could increase your chances of winning a scholarship.

HOW TO GET STARTED

International and domestic students can benefit from a variety of reputable scholarships that are offered by federal and state governments, universities, private institutions, or nonprofit organizations. However, many students are not aware of them. Before applying, you should make sure you have a clear idea of what scholarship you would like to apply for. There are a few things you can do to find a scholarship that would suit your needs.

Talking to your professors is a good idea. Ask them if they know of any opportunities that would be good for you. This strategy worked the best for me. I visited a few professors during their office hours and told them that I wanted to study abroad. I asked if they knew about scholarships that would help me to support myself while studying abroad. Professors get quite a few e-mails from different organizations offering scholarships for their students. Once the professor knows you are interested, he or she can forward you the e-mail.

Another thing that you can do is to look at people's resumes. I found a few interesting scholarships I have never heard of simply by looking at professors' resumes. Maybe there are people in your field that you admire and would like to emulate? Most resumes are available online. Google the names of the people you are interested in and check their resumes. If they are from your university ask them if they would recommend applying to the same scholarship and if they could offer you some advice on how to prepare your application.

A few other strategies include asking the financial aid office at the college you are attending, or plan to attend, talking to your friends, and searching for scholarships online. Asking people working in the financial aid office about opportunities could be quite effective because they might help you to make a list of financial aid resources. Your friends can share their experience in looking for a scholarship, or might know other people who have won a scholarship. Searching for scholarships online can also be beneficial: you can create a list of potential scholarships by using the Internet. The scholarship's website should give you an idea of how and when to apply. However, you have to be very careful in order to avoid scams.

Many scholarships are very competitive, so it is always better to start researching early. It is good to begin to investigate scholarship options when you are still an undergraduate student, or at the beginning of your graduate program. Once you know what kind of scholarship you would like to apply for make sure that you are eligible. Each scholarship has its own requirements. For example, some of the requirements may include citizenship, being able to speak a foreign language, or passing your comprehensive exams. If you meet the criteria, consult the website for specific deadlines. It is extremely important to be well organized. My approach was to mark all the deadlines in my calendar. It is also beneficial to break down the whole process into small, single steps and put the deadlines into your calendar. For example, write down when you are going to work on your personal statement and when you are going to ask for letters of recommendation.

Preparing Documents

Scholarship requirements may vary by institutions but most of them ask for a personal statement, resume, and letters of recommendation. Given that the process of completing all the necessary documents can take a substantial amount of time, it is recommended that you begin the application process as early as possible. Read the instructions carefully before you start preparing all the necessary forms. It's easy to miss some important information and you don't want that to cost you a scholarship. In case you don't understand certain requirements or have a question regarding the forms, contact the scholarship organization. Another piece of advice: send in what the organization requires before the deadline. It may be that you have forgotten to include an important piece of information. This extra time will enable you to resend the application. Remember to make and keep copies of every document you submit.

I recall how overwhelmed I felt when I first applied for a scholarship. The amount of paperwork and time spent on rewriting my personal statement was enormous. However, this whole process taught me a very important skill: I now make a habit of keeping a folder with my resume, which I try to update at least once a year. I also keep all the copies of my GRE and TOEFL scores, as well as my personal and research statements. When I see an opportunity for another scholarship, preparing all the documents takes much less time.

WHAT MAKES A WINNING PERSONAL AND RESEARCH STATEMENT

The personal statement is probably the most important part of your application. Given the competition, even some of the best candidates may not receive the scholarship if they don't stand out from the crowd and catch reviewers' attention. A good personal statement should be written in a way that highlights your strengths and emphasizes your experience. Keep in mind that oftentimes this is the only document where you can demonstrate your skills and prove that you are the best candidate. Therefore, do not wait until the last moment to write your personal statement. It may take a few weeks to write it and make revisions.

There are a few effective strategies for strengthening a personal statement. For example, some scholarship websites offer official guidelines for personal statements. Read carefully how the statement should be prepared. Remember that not only what you describe (your experience, past positions, educational opportunities) but also how you describe it plays a significant role in writing a successful personal statement.

Make sure that you do not make any spelling mistakes and that the format is clean and easy to read. Avoid small font and cluttered spacing, inadequate or poor use of color, paragraphs with multiple numbers in the text, italics, underlining, and long sentences.

Keep in mind that committee members read many personal statements. In order to write a compelling personal statement, use the first paragraph to get their attention. Don't repeat exactly what you included in your resume. Let your resume be a framework within which your personal statement builds a story that connects the dots. For example, why did you decide to be a volunteer? The personal statement is a supplement with which you can illustrate your identity for the committee.

Proofread your statement yourself, but also share it with friends or professors that you trust for constructive comments. You may also want to consult a writing center instructor. People at writing centers will not only proofread your statement, but also explain your errors and help you to fix them. Using outside resources, such as friends and writing centers, can provide an outside opinion on your personal statement, which can help with improving its readability and clarity.

Similar principles apply to your research statement. In my role as a scholarship reviewer, I need to evaluate projects in terms of their originality and feasibility in the proposed timeframe. My experience, however, shows that quite a few applicants forget about the timeframe. When we get excited about our research we tend to think about many aspects, but we must remember to estimate exactly how much time a project will take. Committee members, however, would like to know that you have thought carefully about your research and that your project can be completed within a certain amount of time. I would sit down and think about a few steps that must occur for the project to be complete. How long will it take to collect data? Will you need an institutional review board's (IRB) approval? This timeline need not be detailed, but it should include enough information to give the impression that you are organized and committed to finishing your project. Those who evaluate your project may not be from your area of study and may not understand your field's terminology and jargon, so make sure to be clear and descriptive.

Another key point in your research statement is answering: "so what?" In other words, how can the results from your study be translated into practice? Who will benefit from your research, and how? Reviewers often pay special attention to this section. Ask yourself these questions: How will the project contribute to your field? Will it solve a certain problem? Make sure that you highlight why your project is worthwhile. I review many applications with wonderful theoretical backgrounds, but which lack justifications for their research. If an organization is going to spend money on your scholarship, they will need to make sure that your research will benefit science or society.

LETTERS OF RECOMMENDATION

Most scholarships ask for one or more letters of recommendation. The letters are usually written by your advisor or someone who is familiar with your work. For example, a letter can be written by your supervisor from a place where you volunteer. Time is a crucial factor in preparing an application. You will need to find people who will be willing to write recommendations for you. If you need only one letter, it is usually from your advisor. However, if you need more, you have to carefully choose your recommender. Think about who knows you well and can attest to your skills and qualities listed in your personal statement and resume.

Keep in mind that some professors might be busy and do not have enough time to meet your deadline. My experience has been that some professors need more than 2 weeks to write a letter. Some of them may not know you well enough to be able to write a letter for you. In that case, offer them your resume or write down the main points you would like them to include. You could also try to find someone who knows you better. Most importantly, before you ask a professor to write a letter of recommendation for you, tell him or her what you need it for. Depending on the type of scholarship, he or she will have to emphasize different skills that are suitable.

If you find that your letter is delayed, it may happen that the professor agreed to write the letter for you but then forgot. Send a friendly reminder as the deadline is approaching. You may need to ask your recommender to use their letterhead when writing the letter, as this looks more professional. After receiving a letter of recommendation, do not forget to thank the person who wrote it for you. This person used his or her personal time and helped you by providing one of the most important documents.

After you have completed the process of writing and compiling all of the necessary documents there are a few final steps to take. Prior to submitting your application make sure that you filled in all the blank spaces on the form. Most importantly, remember to sign and date your application, and make a copy of it in case it gets lost in the mail. I would also recommend requesting a return receipt in order to be sure that the organization received it. If you are sending your application via e-mail, kindly request a confirmation that it was received. There are different ways that scholarship organizations process applications. For some organizations this process ends after receiving all the forms. In that case, after you have submitted your application you can relax and wait patiently for the results. However, other organizations, after reviewing your forms, may decide to invite you for an interview. This means that the committee reviewed your application and selected you for the next stage.

HOW TO PREPARE FOR AN INTERVIEW

Some scholarships select applicants based on their documents and then invite them to an interview. The interview may be the most intimidating part of the whole application. Looking back at my experience, I made a few mistakes, and I wish I had been better prepared. However, with time and experience you may gain more confidence. As an applicant, I initially saw an interview as a way for the committee to prove that I lacked the necessary skills and experience to receive a scholarship. At that time, I perceived that the questions they asked seemed to challenge what I wrote in my personal and research statement. Then I realized that this attitude would not take me far.

Interviews serve one main purpose: the interviewee is able to meet the candidate. The committee simply wants to learn more about you. When I read a candidate's personal statement as a review committee member, I always have follow-up questions for the candidate. For example, what made him or her interested in their area of research? Why did he or she change her major? What did he or she learn through volunteering? Think of an interview as a way to introduce yourself in person and to give the committee a chance to know more details about your background rather than an opportunity to grill you.

If you are invited for an interview it means that your application is strong, and that the committee must now make a final decision and choose the best applicant. There are some strategies that can help you to increase your chances of a positive interview.

The most important thing to remember is to make sure you are prepared. The committee may ask you what you know about the scholarship organization. I would strongly advise spending some time finding out when and why the scholarship was established.

It may be that one of the committee members will ask you about your plans for the future. For example, they may want to know your plans after the scholarship is over. Try to think about your future plans so that you are able to tell the committee members in a few sentences what you may be doing in the next few years. You don't have to be specific; for example, you could say that you plan to continue doing research in your area of interest, or that you will apply for a PhD program. However, be sure to make it clear that you have thought about your future.

Another question you may hear is why the committee should choose you. The committee members may want you to justify why you are the best candidate and why you should receive the scholarship. List all your qualities, skills, and goals.

Focus on your strengths and indicate how you might improve other areas that are necessary for a successful recipient of the scholarship. For example, if you are going to study abroad and feel that you need to work on your language skills, make sure that you have a strategy for how you will meet your goals.

Review all the documents that you submitted and make sure that you can talk about your research plan without looking at the paper. You could practice with a friend, imagining that you are telling him or her about your research. Use simple, easy to understand language and see if you can talk about it fluently. Some interviews may be conducted in another language. For example, if you would like to study in Spain, the committee may check your language competency. Practice speaking about your project in a particular language and/or consider taking some private lessons.

A few additional pieces of advice include arriving early, dressing appropriately, and putting your phone on silent. I can't emphasize enough the importance of being punctual: arriving late for your interview can make a bad impression. Additionally, no matter what type of scholarship you are applying for, it is important to be tidy and well groomed. Do not wait until the last minute to prepare your clothes. You may also want to practice while wearing them, which will make you feel more comfortable and decrease your level of anxiety. A final piece of advice that many people tend to forget is to put your phone on silent mode. A vibrating or ringing phone can distract both you and your interviewers.

A PERFECT CANDIDATE

While having a great GPA is beneficial, and sometimes a requirement, academic excellence in scholarship applications is not always enough. There are certain traits that committee members are looking for in candidates. Where the previous sections aimed at helping you to apply for a scholarship from a technical standpoint, this section will briefly describe what factors can make you a strong candidate and increase your chances of receiving a scholarship. Oftentimes these qualities are already reflected in your resume and personal statement. If not, it is never too late to start working on them. The most desired qualities may vary depending on the purpose of the scholarship, but most applicants should have intellectual curiosity, a commitment to improving the lives of others, leadership qualities, and be future-oriented.

Intellectual curiosity is very important because the committee is looking for someone who above all is highly motivated to pursue his or her plans. This factor is almost always more important than your GRE test scores or your GPA. Show that you are passionate not only about your research project but also about life-long learning and improving your skills. You can demonstrate that by, for example, having some extracurricular activities outside of the classroom such as writing for a website or local newspaper or attending workshops.

A commitment to improving the lives of others is also a highly valuable feature. Make sure that your project or your future plans include information on how you would like to help others. You should show the scholarship committee that if they invest in you, they are investing in a person who will contribute to the rest of society.

Scholarship committees look for leaders who know how to be sure of themselves and how to work a few steps ahead. Therefore, it is beneficial if you add this experience to your resume or talk about your leadership skills during the interview.

Being future-oriented is also important because the ability to think about the future will show your dedication and organizational skills. State your short-term and long-term goals and be sure to explain what you have done, and what you plan to do, to realize them.

CONCLUSION

Applying for a scholarship is an exciting experience. In order to avoid stress and feeling overwhelmed, allow yourself enough time to prepare a personal statement, contact professors to provide letters of recommendation for you, and complete other documents that the scholarship organizations require.

Completion of the whole application is time consuming and not an easy process, but once you receive the scholarship, it will have a profound influence on your professional and personal life. The experience of obtaining the scholarship was extremely rewarding for me as it enabled me to meet a lot of interesting people and broaden my area of expertise. I hope it will be the same for you. And if you don't receive a scholarship, don't dwell on it. I didn't receive every scholarship that I applied for, but I treated it as an important lesson and an opportunity to work harder on improving my skills. Sometimes it takes failure to ultimately achieve success.

CHAPTER THREE

Strength in Numbers

Starting and Managing a Dissertation Support Group

DEBRA A. TRUSTY

INTRODUCTION

To use a popular idiom, writing a dissertation is a marathon, not a sprint. Like a marathon, we may find ourselves away from the pack, alone on the trail, and questioning if we are going fast enough or are on the right route. The doubtful little voice in our heads can make us lose our focus and even prevent us from finishing the race. At this crucial point, it helps to have other runners around who can reassure you and inspire you to do your best. The same applies to writing a dissertation: we can drown out that internal voice if we put ourselves among a group of people who are going through the exact same situation, who recognize our accomplishments, and who can remind us that we are capable enough to finish; those real voices that directly counter our negative self-view. The group of people that I refer to is a dissertation support group. In this chapter I will explain the benefits of forming a dissertation support group, suggest a few ways to start your own group, present an outline for structuring your group's meetings, and provide suggestions to personalize the experience for you and your group's members.

INDEPENDENCE, ISOLATION, AND IMPOSTOR SYNDROME

Finishing your comprehensive exams and coursework is a great accomplishment. Best of all, you finally have the chance to strike out on your own and make a contribution to your field! However, the euphoria that comes with the independence to research your own interests is unfortunately accompanied by a major drawback: isolation. Many PhD candidates quickly realize how lonely the process can be without coursework and the daily obligation to sit among their peers (Linder, 2011). Of the students who leave their institution without a PhD, many do so when they begin their dissertation, or when they are in the middle of researching and writing it (Ogden, 2007). This means that graduate students who drop out while they are ABD ("all but dissertation") clearly have the proper knowledge that qualifies them for academic achievement within their respective fields, but lack the resources and stamina they need to finish their degree.

What makes writing a dissertation so hard? The act itself sounds simple, but many of us will find that the timetable is the difficult part. Studies have found that PhD students spend an average of 8 years in their program. If it takes 3 years to become ABD, then, as PhD candidates, we will spend another 5 years writing our dissertations; however, we're doing much more than writing during those years. Depending on the field, we may need to defend a prospectus, conduct research, write grant applications and proposals, and spend a semester, or even several years, at a different institution before ultimately sitting down and writing. Once our hands are on the keyboard, a myriad of stressors may stand in the way: increasing student loan debt, conflicts with an advisor or dissertation committee, difficulties maintaining long-distance romantic relationships, responsibilities of a part-time job, and departmental obligations such as teaching or grading. Without the support network that we had when we were taking courses, we're liable to feel like the only one with these problems and that we are facing them alone.

Isolation fuels the flames of a psychological phenomenon known as impostor syndrome. People with impostor syndrome believe that their success is the result of some sort of deception or trick that they've managed to maintain over the years, and they worry that the truth of their inadequacy will be discovered. It occurs when we let negative "self-talk" take over (Jain, 2002, pp. 14, 24). These are inner thoughts such as "I should have researched this a long time ago," or "my advisor won't agree with anything I'm saying," or (the worst one of all) "I'm never going to finish." Impostor syndrome significantly eats away at our mental resilience. Our internal voice "focuses incessantly on the ways in which we're not smart enough, good enough, or capable enough" (Jain, 2002, p. 24). Often we don't realize that we're practicing negative self-talk until it's spiraled out of control and we consider walking away from graduate school. I haven't met a PhD candidate yet who didn't have this feeling at some point. It's normal—and it shouldn't be.

THE PROACTIVE APPROACH: CREATING A DISSERTATION SUPPORT GROUP

The point of this chapter is not to scare you away from pursuing your PhD. Rather, I've written it in order to empower you during this stressful part of your career path. Dissertation support groups (or DSGs) are self-organized, self-motivated groups that bring fellow ABDs together to discuss aspects of the dissertation experience, such as time management, self-care, and the job application process. This group serves as a medium through which members can keep track of each other's goals, recognize when members are experiencing negative self-talk, and encourage them to correct their self-image. A DSG functions in the same manner as a group therapy session, but without the supervision of a psychiatrist or mental health professional. DSGs also exist in order to offer a sense of community. DSGs are held on a regular schedule, although not as often as an actual course. These meetings serve as "structure to your writing life because you know you will be checking in about your goals and progress" (Linder, 2011, location 435). DGSs also help you avoid others' mistakes. Everyone has his or her own individual approach to or problem with the dissertation process, but not everyone shares it. DSGs create an environment where members can learn about and adopt each other's coping strategies for getting dissertation writing done. DGSs may also help you develop future researching ideas and networking skills. The best DSG will consist of members from several departments and such interdisciplinary groups are always ripe with potential. You'll be surprised by how many excellent brainstorming ideas emerge.

Most importantly, DGSs provide you with support. When the negative self-talk starts to take its toll, giving up seems like the best option. The group, however, inevitably has members who have had the exact same feelings and thoughts and can offer a friendly ear and encouragement. They can help you understand the process, since no one can relate to the challenges of a dissertation more than someone who has either survived the process or is currently experiencing it. They recognize big accomplishments when others might only see small ones.

Making the Group Your Own

Before I provide an outline of my DSG, I want to offer a few important notes. First of all, there are many ways to run a DSG; this chapter presents the approach that has been effective for me and the members of my group. The format that I propose below is a template, not a script or lesson plan. In addition to my format, I also recommend reading Linder's (2011) publication, where she poses questions that will help you design a group that is more individualized.

You need to have personal motivation for leading a DSG. As long as your reason for starting the group is still valid, it is your responsibility to maintain the group and keep consistent communication with members. When you no longer need your DSG, discuss it with the other members to see if someone else wants to become group leader. To avoid this, it may be a good idea to form a group with multiple leaders who rotate responsibilities at meetings. This generates more accountability among members, enables other members to shoulder the work, and creates a communal environment.

Another important note is that you should not place any expectations on group members. Don't demand that members attend every meeting. Be flexible and plan meetings around everyone's schedules, but don't be offended if they don't show up or respond to e-mails. Some people may not have time to attend each meeting and the group will not be productive if members feel obligated to attend.

Finally, and most importantly, leaders need to provide and maintain a positive and optimistic tone that will serve to counter any negative self-talk. As Jain (2002) cautioned, "more often, unfortunately, graduate students have become so accustomed to focusing on their deficits that they find it difficult if not impossible to believe in their strengths" (p. 22). Therefore, the group's collective focus should be on its members' attitudes. A positive tone creates a welcoming, open environment that is conducive to growth and learning. A negative one (that wallows in complaints, gossip, or discouraging remarks about job prospects, for example) inhibits these qualities and may derail members' momentum. Members may need to let off steam or show frustration with the process, but always try to lead the group into a constructive discussion and reinforce the idea that every member has a responsibility to engage in a positive conversation to help resolve issues.

Membership

Everyone in my group is a PhD candidate and actively writing or working on some aspect of his or her dissertation. Roughly 5–10 members are present at any given meeting; I have found that this is an ideal size for maintaining discussion while also providing enough space for anyone to speak. There are many ways to recruit members once you decide to form a group (see Linder, 2011, location 473–495). You can begin by e-mailing your department's listserv, if one is available, or find members while attending department events and activities. Your university may also have resources that you can use: call the graduate school to see if any events take place where you can meet other graduate students. For example, my university's graduate school had a wide range of workshops for grant writing, submitting job applications, and teaching as graduate students. Additionally, I have met several of my group's members through the graduate assistant union, at extracurricular art and exercise classes, and at an honors graduate student society. The most effective way to find members, however, is to ask current members to invite their friends or colleagues. Members are more likely to attend regularly if they know their fellow members and feel comfortable expressing their goals and setbacks.

If possible, look for members within and outside of your department. A moderately interdisciplinary group is extremely beneficial for all members. For example, my group consists of graduate students from departments within the humanities, social sciences, and education: classics, archaeology, English, religion, art history, urban and regional planning, educational psychology and learning systems, and communications. We all have different interests and different levels of experience, which means that each member brings something unique to our meetings. At the same time, however, your members should still come from departments with some similarities. If you are in a humanities-oriented department, for example, I don't recommend organizing a group with graduate students from the STEM fields since the two areas are rather incompatible in terms of timetable and structure. The differences may cause misunderstandings, resentment, and anxiety among group members.

Meeting Structure

My group meets once a month in the evening for about 2 hours. This amount of time is sufficient for everyone to speak about their progress, discuss the topic of the evening, and focus on goal-setting. I strongly recommend that you meet at an off-campus restaurant (but reasonably priced!) for dinner or drinks. These elements help reinforce the idea that this is a social gathering and not a job or a class. There still should be *some* structure, however, so I prepare a handout of the evening's agenda that includes an outline of the topic that will be discussed, members' goals for the previous months, and other items that are described below. This handout helps to keep everyone on task and the conversation moving.

Each meeting begins with (re)introductions, where members briefly share where they are in the dissertation process and (if they were at the previous meeting) what goals they accomplished in the past month. We always set monthly goals at the end of each meeting, so I like to have a list of everyone's previous month's goals on the agenda in order to refresh our memories. If a member has met his or her goal, be sure that the group offers plenty of praise, even if it seems like a simple or small achievement. It's hard for many graduate students to recognize an achievement when they are intensely focused on the long-term goal, which is when a DSG can become extremely invaluable. If members don't meet their goals, don't make them feel guilty. Chances are good that their inner voice has been doing that all month, so why should you join in? This is another instance where the group should be supportive and remind each other that small setbacks are learning experiences. Engage in a constructive discussion with the entire group. Allow enough time for the group to brainstorm on ways that the member can refocus or approach a problem from a new direction. The most important function of this group is to create a positive environment.

After reviewing our goals, we move on to the main topic of the meeting, which was chosen at the end of the previous meeting. This subject typically deals with a problem or concern that one or more group members currently have. As the leader, I present the topic like a book report, using information gathered from many resources, including those listed in the table. I also provide a brief outline within the handout that highlights specific suggestions and ideas. For example, the main topic in the template is about refocusing after winter or summer break. Within the outline, I list three main points: preparing yourself, preparing your materials, and preparing your environment. Within those points are suggestions such as "create multiple schedules" and "reserve times of the day for different activities," which were collected from Linder (2011, location 72) and Jain (2002, p. 30). During group discussion I then elaborate on each of these points and allow group members to make additional suggestions or comments.

After a discussion on the main topic, we begin to wrap up the meeting. The first step is to ask all participants to set a goal for the following month. This can be a goal for any part of the dissertation process, such as reading, research, or writing, but I always encourage members to make SMART goals: Specific, Measurable, Attainable, Relevant, and Time-bound (Doran, 1981). If a member didn't meet last month's goal, it's a good opportunity to remind him or her about this technique since it is linked to higher success rates. I provide space on the handout for members to record each other's goals in order to solidify the members' decision to reach a specific goal. This also seems to serve as a subconscious, informal obligation among the members of the group. When members set goals, I ask if they would like someone in the group to check in with them throughout the month and remind them of their goal(s). We call this person a "disser-buddy," since they function in the same way as a buddy system, creating accountability between members. If they ask for a disser-buddy I wait for volunteers rather than assigning someone. The volunteer then establishes details with the other member and decide how frequently they will contact each other. These can simply be text messages, e-mails, or phone calls to see if the member is staying on task.

Afterwards, we select a topic for next month's meeting based on any conversation that has come up during the evening (see the table below for a few examples). I also like to include a list of activities that are taking place in town over the next month such as university events, professional development opportunities, and entertainment or non-academic events, such as concerts or festivals. This serves as a visual example of the range of opportunities that exist for members to become more involved in-between meetings.

Our meeting concludes with a personal, silent reflection at the end of the prepared handout that asks four questions: "What did we discuss?" "What did I learn?" "How can I apply it to my dissertation?," and "What questions do I still have?" The personal reflection is meant to solidify discussions or ideas that occurred during the meeting and can also serve as a "notes" section. Members do not turn this in as if it were an assignment or homework, but keep it for their own personal reference as many people keep their handouts over the entire course of their candidacy.

ADDITIONAL SUGGESTIONS

Beyond the basic outline of DSGs that I have provided in this chapter, there are several options that you can add to your own group. The first is a writing feedback circle that promotes in-group writing. This activity requires that each member bring a paragraph from his or her dissertation to share with the group's members. Everyone's writing segments are passed around the group so that members can write suggestions, questions, or corrections. This activity ensures that everyone receives some sort of immediate feedback. This is great for members who are experiencing writer's block, but it may take up a significant amount of time if you are also planning to discuss a topic.

Possible Meeting Topics

- Grant-writing and personal budget management
- Isolation, "impostor syndrome," and self-care
- Job applications and interviews
- Networking and socialization in academia
- Physically and mentally preparing to write
- Practicing mindfulness
- Publishing and delivering papers in graduate school
- Time management, goal setting, and multitasking responsibilities
- University's formatting and clearance process
- Writer's block and staying motivated

Long-term projects can also be implemented in your group. For example, my group tracked the evolution of our workspaces over a semester to see if there was some sort of pattern we found helpful or productive. You may also want to keep track of the number of goals that have been completed over the year and ask the group to reward the members with the best record by buying them dessert at the final meeting. Guest speakers are also effective additions to a group. Invite someone to attend a meeting and ask him or her to offer expertise on a certain topic. You can ask someone who has recently finished their dissertation to talk about their defense or the university's requirements for graduating. I have also asked newly hired tenure-track faculty members to speak about job applications and interviews. These speakers can provide up-to-date and sage advice that you as a leader would not be able to discuss as fully.

It might also be useful to organize a few activities outside of meetings (or ask a fellow member to do so!). Several of my group members took it upon themselves to meet once a week at a coffeehouse for writing sessions. They simply sit together and write, engaging in productive socialization. Additionally, members may find it advantageous to present their research to each other as an informal talk to prepare for a prospectus or dissertation defense. Relaxing events such as walking or exercise groups and movie dates are also good ideas. All of these suggestions serve as supplementary opportunities to engage in more social (but often still productive) activities.

As you can see, many helpful practices and traditions have emerged from my group's DSG meetings, and this chapter is my way of offering thanks to each of them. From this experience the PhD candidates in my group have gained insights into efficient study habits, learned from each other's mistakes and victories, and received constructive criticism to improve their writing. Most importantly, each of us has found a supportive community that helps us realize that we aren't alone in this difficult journey. By using this outline to form your own dissertation group, you can find the same: a pack of runners who will watch you cross the finish line of the longest marathon of your career.

REFERENCES

Doran, G. T. (1981). There's a S.M.A.R.T. way to write management's goals and objectives. *Management Review (AMA FORUM)* 70(11), 35–36.

Jain, R. D. (2002). *Get it done faster: Secrets of dissertation success.* Gaithersburg, MD: Moonswept Press.

Linder, K. (2011). *To do: Dissertation* [Kindle edition]. ASIN: B00589WJD4. Retrieved from http://www.amazon.com/To-Do-Dissertation-ebook/dp/B00589WJD4/

Ogden, E. H. (2007). *Complete your dissertation or thesis in two semesters or less.* Lanham, MD: Rowman & Littlefield.

CHAPTER FOUR

How to Turn a Good Relationship with Your Supervisor into a Great One

JU SEONG LEE

INTRODUCTION

The relationship between the supervisor and the graduate student is one of the key determinants for successful graduate study. A good supervisory relationship ideally helps prospective graduate students adjust to the graduate program, helps students avoid slow academic progress while reducing the school attrition rate for current graduate students, and prepares them for the job market following graduation.

The aim of this chapter is to offer straightforward, practical advice on how to maintain a positive relationship with your supervisor. This chapter will offer steps for selecting the right academic supervisor; practical tips for facilitating personal and professional relationships with your supervisor; and a list of academic supervisors' perceptions of their favorite (or preferred) graduate students. In addition, this chapter will offer a special section for international students for whom English is their second/foreign language. In this section, the international student can learn how to cope with several challenges commonly experienced by the international graduate students in the United States—in particular, how to mitigate (and resolve) typical transcultural misunderstandings with your American supervisor.

SELECTING THE RIGHT SUPERVISOR

Finding the right supervisor, just like finding the right spouse, is one of the most important steps for successful graduate school life. In this section, I discuss five steps for selecting the right supervisor. These are identifying yourself, searching for the graduate programs and professors that would be the best fit for you, contacting the potential supervisors, figuring out his or her personality and working style, and maintaining a good relationship through your constant personal endeavor.

Identifying yourself (e.g., research interest, motivation, working style) is a key part of selecting the right supervisor. I kept asking myself the following questions before I applied to a doctoral program: Why should I get a degree? What will I do with it? What topics fascinate me? What is my passion? Am I motivated to do this? Is this really the path I want to follow in life? After answering these questions, I reached the conclusion that I wanted to become a faculty member, with a specialization in transcultural and foreign language education, in one of the top doctoral programs in the United States.

I started asking other Korean professors, colleagues (undergraduate), seniors, and friends about the right graduate program(s) and potential supervisor(s) that would correspond with my personal and academic interests. I even attended an academic conference hosted in Seoul to talk with one of the presenters whose PhD program was being undertaken at one of my potential candidate schools. I also tried to get relevant information from the school website. It took me nearly three months of searching for and sorting through the right programs and supervisors. I found four potential supervisors who were all well respected in their field. Then I looked carefully at whether the graduate program where they worked would be the best fit for me. This match is very important.

I contacted the four American professors via e-mail, enclosing my CV and personal statement, including my purpose of study and research interests. Fortunately, all of them answered me back positively, but one particular professor showed great interest in me. We exchanged a few more e-mails and ended up having a Skype interview. After nearly 50 minutes of conversation, he followed up by sending me his CV, his published academic papers, and his current Fulbright project proposal. He would eventually become my current supervisor. Later, he told me that among other factors, he decided to contact me because I had interests in teaching and in qualitative research that were closely aligned with his. In searching for a prospective supervisor talk about your research interests with potential supervisors before applying to the graduate program.

After finding my potential supervisor, I tried to figure out his personality and working style. Fortunately, my supervisor took the initiative by asking four of his former/current PhD students to write me e-mails about him and the PhD program. For my part, as a new research assistant I also took a proactive role in deciding to travel to Morocco with my supervisor, at my own expense, to help him plan his Fulbright project. I thought it would be a great opportunity for us to get to know each other. For nearly two weeks we spent most of our time together engaging in diverse activities in various contexts.

While I was with him I attended the talks he gave and observed the way he interacted with other professors and students in various formal and informal settings. When we were eating, or drinking tea, I usually asked him a lot of questions about his coursework, research/projects, working style, and expectations about graduate students. In most of our leisure time, we shared many life stories. After this trip I felt confident that he and I could get along well for the next 5 years. Most of all, as a result of this professional trip I could assimilate more smoothly into the new institution because through our interactions my supervisor gave me an insightful overview of graduate school life, coursework, research, and general living situations. Although you may not be able to fly to exotic locations to work with a potential supervisor, proactively approach your supervisor and learn more about his or her personality and working style (and get involved in his or her projects) if the supervisor is assigned before you begin your PhD program.

Even after you believe you've chosen the right supervisor, it's important to keep in mind that maintaining this relationship is going to require constant personal endeavor on your part. In addition to engaging in his Morocco project, I tried to take the initiative in organizing meetings with my supervisor on a regular basis and discussed diverse ideas that helped formulate my early research and a dissertation topic in the early stages of my PhD study. I also decided to travel to Colorado for 10 days to take part in his service-learning project. I believed I would learn new skills while deepening our personal relationship. As previously mentioned, that is why you should be very excited about what your supervisor is doing because you can benefit by becoming involved in some of his or her work(s) after you've entered the graduate program.

However, it is important to remember that some graduate students may have an advisor assigned to them after entering or spending one year in a given graduate program. It all depends on how the program is set up in your school, so investigate your degree of choice when you search for the right program and school.

FACILITATING A PERSONAL AND PROFESSIONAL RELATIONSHIP WITH YOUR SUPERVISOR

It is often said that married life is much more essential than a mere wedding event. The same is true for the supervisor/student relationship. After selecting the right supervisor it's time to consider how you can maintain the good relationship, or even turn a good relationship into a better one. In this section I discuss practical tips for facilitating a personal and professional relationship with the supervisor.

It is important to get to know your supervisor's personal and professional styles as quickly as possible. I still remember that I intentionally spent a great portion of time trying to identify just *who* my supervisor was and what he valued the most. In doing this I tried to observe how he approached his work and how he interacted with undergraduate and graduate students. I also asked his current and former doctoral students about him, which often gave me new, diverse perspectives.

But I learned something else about him after going through some periods of trial and error too. For example, it took a few months to realize that he would want to read a complete version of a paper or document so that he would not be giving me feedback on an ongoing—and therefore incomplete—paper. After I realized that was his style, I began to e-mail him complete works only. But in the beginning, when I was not adequately aware of his working style, it was embarrassing and even frustrating when I didn't get the answer back from him that I expected. I could have saved myself some effort by simply having a frank discussion with him at the beginning of our relationship.

It is important to interact with your supervisor as often as possible. The beginning stage of your graduate study is particularly crucial. For instance, I tried to get to know my supervisor personally and professionally through various communication channels. Before entering the PhD program, we often used e-mail for exchanging ideas. Then, we employed Skype for video calls and chatting. At some point, especially after we spent 2 weeks in Morocco together, Facebook became a major tool for connecting us. After I arrived on campus, we often conversed via phone calls or text messages. Apart from these communication devices, we spent a lot of time off campus, in more varied, and sometimes casual, activities such as going to the gym, dining out, professional trips to other states and overseas, having meals at his home, cycling, going for groceries, watching his son's soccer games, going to the airport, and drinking coffee/beer. Admittedly, most students don't have such an intimate relationship with their supervisors, but the point is to see the relationship as potentially larger than one based solely upon a thesis.

This casual time is important, and you need to take advantage of it. Early this year, when one of my supervisor's new students from Turkey came to the campus, we drove to the international airport to pick him up together. On the way to the airport, we talked with each other, non-stop, for nearly three hours. In this casual way, most of the major decisions (for example, coursework, projects, publications) were discussed, and, at times, decisions reached. Even today, we don't schedule regular meeting times because both of us prefer informal settings, and we often have conversations in informal settings. It can be vital to engage in and develop a personal relationship with your new supervisor at the beginning stage of your graduate study, and, subsequently, to figure out how you can creatively maximize this type of interaction with your supervisor.

Also, participate in your supervisor's work. As I wrote earlier, I travelled to Morocco to work with him in planning his Fulbright Senior Scholar project, in addition to his 2-week-long service-learning project in Colorado. Now I am assisting him as a teaching assistant (TA) for his undergraduate course. I've found that one of the greatest benefits I can attain is by virtue of developing both a personal and professional relationship with my supervisor. By becoming involved in his work, I could spend an ample amount of time with my supervisor, developing my personal relationship with him as a colleague, while getting direction, advice, and feedback related to my academic and professional issues. That's why it is important to choose a potential academic supervisor whose research areas are aligned with yours.

SUPERVISORS' PERCEPTIONS OF THEIR "FAVORITE" STUDENTS

You may get more useful insights if you can understand this issue from the supervisors' perspective. I conducted informal interviews with three faculty members on how they perceive their favorite graduate advisee. In this section, I discuss those points most frequently mentioned during these interviews.

Every supervisor unanimously preferred students whose research interests were closely aligned with their own. My supervisor, for instance, usually receives two e-mails a week from prospective graduate students regarding the graduate school program, as well as the possibility (or availability) of him being their potential supervisor. He flatly ignores most of these inquiry e-mails because their research interests don't closely correspond to his own. He tends to pay more attention to the potential (or current) graduate students whose research areas are matched with his own. Although you may get accepted into the program due to other strong factors (such as a high GPA/GRE, or funding), it's still crucial to choose a topic that your supervisor may find interesting or at least relevant to his or her own research areas, a supervisor aligned with your research interest.

Several years before my supervisor had accepted a male international doctoral student as his student, after exchanging e-mails and realizing their research interests were seemingly compatible. After the student arrived on campus, however, they did not get along at all because the student was very quantitative in his methods and very fixed in his perspective, whereas my supervisor was qualitative-oriented. After my supervisor had a few very difficult meetings with the student, he eventually urged the student to find a new supervisor in another program that turned out to be a perfect fit. My supervisor later commented that it was difficult for both he and the student, simply because their research was not a good match.

Supervisors tend to favor students who are productive in their writing. This advice is particularly applicable to PhD students. Most supervisors emphasize that graduate students (especially those who want to work in academia) need to think from a long-term perspective, beyond their PhD dissertation stage all the way into a faculty job. Among other criteria, scholarly work (or publications), which produces an adequate volume of academic papers in terms of quality and quantity, plays an integral part in securing a job in the market place (or in academia). One of the common mistakes PhD students make, according to one senior professor I interviewed, is their tendency to first collect data in their third or fourth year of the PhD period and then wait. Then they start analyzing and writing it up in the fourth or fifth year. This is not a recommended approach, however, because it may take longer than anticipated to complete the work due to a series of unexpected life interruptions or delays. As a result, a large number of doctoral students can't graduate due to unanticipated delays, which result in unfinished dissertation work. Supervisors prefer to have students who can consistently write papers from day one. To put it simply, having students who are disciplined, effective writers makes a supervisor's life much easier.

Supervisors want their students to understand their expectations. Otherwise, it could cause discord or conflict. As I mentioned above, at the beginning stage of my doctoral study I sent my supervisor an incomplete, in-progress paper for his feedback, but he did not respond to it. It was very strange for me because he usually answered my e-mails instantly. The same thing happened repeatedly— me e-mailing him but not receiving a response. Later he told me that he wanted his students to send him a complete paper, not an ongoing, five-page paper, for example. He expected to see the whole forest (a complete paper), not the trees (the parts of the paper). Another example is the frequency of organizing meetings between a supervisor and student. In the beginning, I insisted on meeting with my supervisor as often as possible. Back then I did not know how busy a faculty member was. Of course, having a regular meeting motivated me to make continued progress and keep my supervisor aware of my work, but my supervisor preferred (or expected) me to bring the final results of my work (summaries of related work and experimental or analytical results), not the work-in-progress.

Another critical factor in graduate study is the degree of independence. Students must bear in mind that it is *their* graduate degree, not the supervisor's. My supervisor emphasizes this point over and over—that I should become an independent researcher, not entirely dependent on him. I took this to mean that I should become proactive and know what I want to do and how I want to go about doing it. However, other supervisors may have different expectations in this regard. It is important to notice as soon as possible what a supervisor expects from a student. Talking with other graduate students may give you some ideas about what your supervisor expects from you, and I would encourage you to do so as well.

SPECIAL TIPS FOR INTERNATIONAL STUDENTS

International students face unique problems in U.S. higher education (Andrade, 2006; Gebhard, 2012; Huang, 2004; Huang & Brown, 2009; Li, Wang, & Xiao, 2014; Lin & Scherz, 2014). Based on the above literature, as well as my firsthand experience as an international student from Korea, I offer in this section some useful tips for international students who intend to study at (or are currently enrolled in) an American graduate school.

Treat a supervisor like a colleague. From my experience, a majority of Asian graduate students, including my earlier self, expect their American supervisors to become their "scholarly fathers or mothers" due to the influence of Confucian philosophy and home culture (Huang, 2004; Huang & Brown, 2009). They tend to wait for their American supervisors to come to find and push them. However, you need to take the initiative in this relationship by asking questions, advancing ideas, challenging assumptions, or showing interest and support for shared goals as a "junior colleague" instead of relying entirely on your supervisor. In the United States, unlike in Asian (or other countries') cultures, supervisors don't always assume the position of being the student's mentors. Students have a great deal of freedom to choose what they want to work on. Of course, supervisors play a role in giving advice and guidance and checking whether students are progressing and moving forward in meeting academic standards. But you can disagree with your supervisor on a certain topic, and that is understood to be acceptable. It is important not to be afraid to voice your opinion and viewpoints. American supervisors may not see you as merely a student; they view you as a potential scholar.

It is helpful to know fellow graduate students of the same nationality. In my first semester of my PhD study, when everything was new, my Korean colleagues helped me tremendously with my academic challenges (classes to take, exams to prepare for), sociocultural issues (cultural shock/fatigue, adjusting to new cultural norms, new situations on campus), and general living (getting around, even buying groceries). These were things my American supervisor could hardly help me with. During your graduate work, friends or colleagues of the same nationality can become great resources to help you deal with unexpected personal problems or life conflicts that your American supervisor would not sympathize with or understand.

Last but not least, a conflict may occur between you and your American supervisor. It has been repeatedly reported that many graduate students leave the program or transfer to another school because of a conflict with their supervisor. Deal with any conflict as soon as possible, while maintaining a positive, professional relationship. From my experience, a conflict between supervisor and (domestic or international) student likely arises out of a misunderstanding. As in any good relationship, it is important to clear up misunderstandings quickly; otherwise they can negatively affect your personal and academic life. When I have conflicting opinions, I try my best to minimize any misunderstanding pertaining to the situation. I always write down my objections or concerns first before meeting with my supervisor. In the subsequent meeting I then address my concerns as clearly and accurately as possible, based on my written notes—on the assumption that my supervisor may have no prior knowledge or experience in Asian culture, or my own previous personal experience. International students can build a healthy relationship simply by avoiding miscommunication or misunderstanding—and by being proactive about communicating.

CONCLUSION

Building up and maintaining a good relationship with your supervisor is a key component of succeeding in graduate school. Take the initiative to develop more intimate personal and professional relationships, strive to create a supportive environment, and practice more effective communication. These elements will make your graduate school life a very enjoyable experience.

Prospective graduate students should realize that the roles a professor plays during the undergraduate years are different from those during a period of graduate study. During graduate study, the supervisor-student relationship tends to be more difficult than the beginning graduate student may anticipate. But it is possible to turn your relationship with your supervisor into a great one and successfully navigate your way through a rewarding graduate school experience in the United States.

REFERENCES

Andrade, M. S. (2006). International students in English-speaking universities: Adjustment factors. *Journal of Research in International Education, 5*(2), 131–154.
Gebhard, J. G. (2012). International students' adjustment problems and behaviors. *Journal of International Students, 2*(2), 184–193.

Huang, J. (2004). Voices from Chinese students: Professors' use of English affects academic listening. *College Student Journal, 38*(2), 212–223.

Huang, J., & Brown, K. (2009). Cultural factors affecting Chinese ESL students' academic learning. *Education, 129*(4), 643–653.

Li, J., Wang, Y., & Xiao, F. (2014). East Asian international students and psychological well-being: A systematic review. *Journal of International Students, 4*(4), 301–313.

Lin, S.-Y., & Scherz, S. D. (2014). Challenges facing Asian international graduate students in the US: Pedagogical considerations in higher education. *Journal of International Students, 4*(1), 16–33.

PART TWO

The Flourishing Academic

CHAPTER FIVE

Scholarly Publication

A Multilingual Perspective

ATSUSHI IIDA

INTRODUCTION

Writing for scholarly publication is an important academic and professional activity. From a scholar's standpoint, the purpose of academic publication is to present and share their research and knowledge with other researchers. This scholarly activity is indispensable for the process of professional career development. Scholarly publication is also crucial for graduate students. Academic publication is regarded as one of the requirements to receive a scholarship for doctoral studies, win a research grant sponsored by some organizations, and apply for a full-time teaching position in higher education. Academic publishing helps graduate students to develop their scholarship and provides various possibilities for their future career.

It was at the end of my second semester in the doctoral program that I sent my first manuscript for a journal. At that time, I had no idea what to do for scholarly writing because I had never taken a course such as "academic publication" or "writing for scholarly publication" in the program. In addition to my lack of experience and low self-esteem, my identities as a non-native English speaker, an English as a second language (ESL) graduate student, and a novice writer prevented me from submitting my manuscript to an English-medium journal.

This chapter discusses my struggles and challenges with scholarly publication, as a graduate student, but also as a multilingual student. This chapter is written for both the domestic and international student. Reflecting on my personal experiences, I describe several key issues of writing for scholarly publication and propose practical guidelines for others, focusing on the most typical publication type, research articles.

CHALLENGES AND ISSUES OF SCHOLARLY WRITING

I published 10 research articles and two book reviews in national and international journals during my doctoral studies. Many of my published papers started from term papers that I worked on in the doctoral program. As a graduate student, I had several key issues in the process of writing for scholarly publication.

Peer Review

The first issue surfaced because of my own misunderstanding concerning academic publishing. When I enrolled in the doctoral program, I had two major misunderstandings about scholarly publication: only famous or "big name" researchers can publish their work in academic journals, and non-native international graduate students have no chance of being published in English-mediated journals. However, this is not true, and the chances of publication are equal for all researchers.

Many high-indexed and qualified journals employ a refereed and peer-reviewed system through which a few editorial board members review one manuscript with no identifying information pertaining to the author. Although many reviewers imagine different aspects of the writer's identity such as his or her language background or nationality in the review process (Tardy & Matsuda, 2009), they cannot identify exactly who wrote the manuscript. This blind review maintains the quality and reliability of each academic journal and provides researchers with equal opportunities for publishing their work. This means that regardless of our academic status (e.g., graduate student or full professor) or nationality (e.g., native or non-native English speaker), our work will be published if it meets the publication standards of the journal.

Genre Knowledge

The second issue that I faced in the publication process is related to a lack of genre knowledge. I had not been taught the concept of genres in English as a foreign language (EFL) writing courses in my native country, Japan. Nor had I been taught it explicitly, even in the graduate program. My lack of genre knowledge often prevented me from having a natural flow in my written communication.

Especially, such issues as inaccurate word choice, strange paper organization, awkward transition, or inappropriate tone of writing made it difficult for both the journal editor and reviewers to understand my arguments. As a consequence, it caused miscommunication between us. As discussed in second language writing research, genre knowledge is regarded as one of the most important components for active and successful communication as experts, and writers must develop the knowledge in the academic field (Hyland, 2009; Tardy, 2009). Academic publishing is a disciplinarily situated practice, so we need to understand and learn an appropriate way to communicate messages in that written form.

Developing Familiarity/Expertise with Style Guides

We can easily imagine that writing styles in the social sciences are different from those in the natural sciences, but scholars need to use different writing formats for their research papers even within one discipline; for example, while APA (American Psychology Association) style is used in much of the humanities, scholars in English literature use MLA (Modern Language Association) style. Even in one specific area of English language teaching, I sometimes had to use Chicago Style to adhere to the submission guidelines for a target journal. Since each journal may employ a different set of guidelines, we need to understand its expectation and apply it to our manuscript in order to communicate appropriately in a specific disciplinary discourse community. Otherwise, it will not be accepted by the target journal.

Choosing Suitable Journals

Each academic journal has its own scope, aim, and target audience, which is clearly described on the journal's website. As graduate students we must consider these factors when preparing manuscripts. From my experience, I find it important to be aware of audience. Scholarly publication is a disciplinarily situated literacy practice, and our message is for someone else in a particular discourse community. If we have a different audience, our arguments in the manuscript will change. When I sent out my manuscript for an international journal, I received feedback from the editor and was asked to broaden it out to have a wider audience. This meant that my paper was too focused and targeted only a particular context. The editor found it more meaningful for me to revise my manuscript so that English teachers around the world could read it and apply some of the ideas to their teaching, rather than only focusing on a group of teachers in one country. I would not have received this type of feedback if I had submitted it to a domestic journal published in Japan. This experience illustrates the significance of developing awareness of audience in the publication process in addition to making a strong connection between the content of our manuscript and the aim of the target journal. There remains an issue of how widely or narrowly our manuscript broadens, but we need to determine a specific group of readers in preparation for publication.

English Language Conventions

This issue comes from both personal and cultural phases, but it is closely related to each graduate student's language proficiency (Manchón, 2011), rhetorical knowledge (Casanave, 2004; Paltridge et al., 2009), and language writing experiences (Leki, 2011; Sasaki, 2009). In my case, as a second-language writer, I often received feedback from reviewers that my paper was wordy and its redundancy made it difficult for them to follow my arguments. As discussed in Rinnert and Kobayashi (2009), this might be attributed to my lack of English linguistic and rhetorical knowledge or/and transfer of Japanese knowledge to English writing. However, I always attempted to follow English language conventions and modify my paper in a disciplinarily appropriate manner. While working on my revision, I read and analyzed several journal articles published by scholars in my area of research (e.g., applied linguistics, TESOL, second language writing) and applied their organizational patterns and rhetorical rules to my English writing. Doing so enabled me to understand communicative functions in academic writing and develop my academic literacy. This advice is pertinent to those whose first language is English, as academic conventions can appear as a "foreign" language when beginning graduate studies.

PRACTICAL GUIDELINES: WRITING RESEARCH ARTICLES FOR PUBLICATION

The most typical publication type is a research article that discusses a specific topic in an academic field, including extended research and commentary. Many scholars have shared their studies by publishing their research articles and contributed to the development of academic disciplines. In this sense, publishing research papers is a crucial academic and professional activity for those who study and teach in academic institutions.

In graduate school, students are often assigned to write research papers as a course requirement. While attending their regular lessons, they are expected to work on their own research outside the classroom and submit their papers to the course instructor. Such assignments are time-consuming and challenging to most graduate students. Considering the time and effort required to complete this task, it would be great if this literacy practice could lead to scholarly publication, and the practical guidelines offered below will point out how to do this. Initial research work can also provide material for publication. Below are five steps to prepare coursework and initial research material for journal submission.

Step 1: Preparation of Term Papers and Initial Research

Even though graduate students can finish and submit their own research paper to the course instructor, it does not necessarily mean that they are ready to send it out to a journal. While a research paper may meet expectations as a course assignment, it might not always fit the scope and aim of an academic journal. So, you'll most likely need to revise your term paper to meet the journal submission guidelines.

At this stage, it is worth exploring the differences between theory-generating, empirical studies and literature reviews. While literature reviews are not regarded as full research papers and have no consideration for publication, they can be reframed to present something new to the field—such as your unique interpretation of the literature. Generally, it is easier to publish theory-generating inquiry or empirical research papers. Many academic journals, though not all, invite contributors to submit empirical research papers. If the term paper or aspect of your research is based on the development of theoretical arguments, you will need to find a journal that accepts theoretical papers.

Step 2: Targeting Journals

Choosing suitable journals can be challenging. No matter how well written your research paper might be, it won't stand a chance if it's sent to the wrong journal.

Therefore, an effective approach to find a suitable journal is to go back to a list of references in your work and review which journal articles you used in the paper. This process enables you to understand the connection of the paper to a specific journal. You may want to select one specific journal for the submission at this stage, but I recommend that you choose three to five journals. You can then rank these from high-prestige (or high-impact factor) to low-prestige (or low-impact factor) journals, and try to submit your manuscript to the most challenging and then the least difficult journal. Doing so can enable you to send it to the next journal quite soon after it has been rejected by the previous journal, after having incorporated the feedback from the reviewers of that initial submission.

Another useful approach is to ask experienced researchers for advice. Graduate students have a lot of chances to discuss their research with several professors and classmates in their program. Using these opportunities enables you not only to understand where to submit your manuscript but also to recognize what to do for submission. Getting advice helps you to have a clear vision for academic publishing and to get ready to work on scholarly writing. At this stage, you will need to visit each of the listed journals' websites, read the submission guidelines carefully, and confirm how the content of your work suits the scope, aim, and target audience of the journal in order to make a final decision on where to submit your paper.

Step 3: Turning Term Papers or Initial Research into Manuscripts for the Journal

After choosing a journal for the submission, start to revise your papers according to the submission guidelines, with careful consideration to readership. Since a manuscript that does not meet the journal submission requirement will be rejected, you need to prepare it following the submission guidelines. Read back issues of the journal and analyze several articles. I have found this activity effective in terms of developing genre knowledge on research papers. Reading and analyzing previously published papers enables you to understand the format, style, and organization of the journal articles.

Writing research papers is a form of academic literacy practice through which scholars share their studies and knowledge in a disciplinarily appropriate manner in a particular discourse community. Of particular importance in this professional activity is understanding and learning to use the genre knowledge for the successful written communication. From this viewpoint, it is useful for novice researchers to read, analyze, and appreciate the content and structure of each journal article. This task enables you not only to develop a greater sense of genre but also to recognize how to work on your manuscripts. In so doing you can overcome organizational and structural problems in turning your term papers into manuscripts for the journal.

In addition, you must work on the quality of your manuscript. Find experienced researchers (e.g., advisors, professors, or classmates) to read the finished draft and offer their constructive feedback. This provides an opportunity to discuss your study, revise the manuscript based on the feedback, and polish it for submission. Through this revision process you can receive an initial review of the manuscript before a journal editor and editorial board members actually review it. In so doing, you can improve the quality of your manuscript and get it ready for submission to the journal.

Step 4: Submission to the Journal

The key perspective of scholarly publication is for each scholar to make contributions to academia by sharing new research findings, theories, or knowledge with others in a specific discipline. It does not matter whether a contributor is a native or non-native English speaker, or whether he or she is a tenured professor or graduate student. Of particular importance in submitting a manuscript is explaining in the cover letter to the editor the purpose and significance of the current study and its potential contribution to the journal. It is also crucial to suggest how marketable the manuscript is to the editor. This may be an unfamiliar task to students in graduate programs, but you are required to develop and learn to use skills to explain your study in a succinct and appropriate manner in scholarly publishing.

Step 5: Negotiation with a Journal Editor

After submitting a manuscript you must then wait to hear the editor's decision on the manuscript submission. It usually takes approximately 12 to 16 weeks to finish reviewing a manuscript, depending on the journal.

Once your manuscript is accepted, you will be able start to work with the editor's guidance. If it is accepted with revisions, you will need to modify and resubmit it on the basis of the reviewers' comments. At this point you will need to decide which comments to use and how to reflect the points in the revision. If the manuscript needs minor revisions, you may be able to respond to the reviewers' comments. However, if it needs major revisions and each reviewer provides different suggestions, it would be difficult to follow all of their points. In this case, you should keep in mind that you always have access to the editor and should feel free to ask questions, share problems, and request some solutions for the revision. From my experience, it's better for the author to explain to the editor what changes will be made in resubmitting the manuscript; in this way, both the editor and reviewers can easily understand the progress of the paper and their review process will go smoother.

If the manuscript is rejected you should not be disappointed at the result. It is challenging even for experienced researchers to get their work published in a peer-reviewed journal. Since the manuscript will have been reviewed by a couple of experts in the academic field, you should carefully read their feedback, identify the paper's problems, and modify it for submission to another journal. For the next submission, you will have to follow another submission guideline, but the quality of the manuscript should now be better than the original one. Even if you receive a rejection letter from the editor, you can still learn a lot from the publication process and can polish your manuscripts in response to reviewer comments.

CONCLUSION

Scholarly publication is an important academic literacy practice. Some students may need to publish their work as a graduation requirement; others will need to publish their papers if they are planning to apply for a full-time or tenure-track position at the tertiary level. While publication may be a time-consuming and challenging task to graduate students, I believe that this literacy practice helps each student to develop a sense of authorship and become a more engaged writer.

As for scholarly publication, if we don't submit our manuscripts, they'll never get published. I strongly encourage graduate students to gain awareness of academic publishing and attempt to submit their work to peer-reviewed journals. Regardless of the result of a paper submission, you can benefit from that experience, and the knowledge, processes, and strategies of academic publishing can be applied to the future scholarly activity. Scholarly writing enables you to understand the meaning of learning in academia and reflect on how, as a researcher, you situate yourself and what contributions you can make in your specific disciplinary discourse community.

REFERENCES

Casanave, C. P. (2004). *Controversies in second language writing: Dilemmas and decisions in research and instruction.* Ann Arbor, MI: University of Michigan Press.

Curry, M. J., & Lillis, T. (2013). *A scholar's guide to getting published in English: Critical choices and practical strategies.* Bristol, England: Multilingual Matters.

Flowerdew, J. (2008). The non-Anglophone scholar on the periphery of scholarly publication. *AILA Review: Linguistic Inequality in Scientific Communication Today, 20,* 14–27.

Hyland, K. (2009). *Academic discourse.* London, England: Continuum.

Iida, A. (2011, June 9–11). *Scholarly publication for NNES graduate students: Challenges and issues.* Paper presented at the meeting of Symposium on Second Language Writing, Taipei, Taiwan.

Leki, I. (2011). Learning to write in a second language: Multilingual graduates and undergraduates expanding genre repertoires. In R. M. Manchón (Ed.), *Learning-to-write and writing-to-learn in an additional language* (pp. 85–106). Amsterdam, The Netherlands: John Benjamins.

Li, Y. (2007). Apprentice scholarly writing in a community of practice: An intraview of an NNES graduate student writing a research article. *TESOL Quarterly, 41,* 55–79.

Lillis, T., & Curry, M. J. (2010). *Academic writing in a global context: The politics and publishing in English.* New York, NY: Routledge.

Manchón, R. M. (2011). Writing to learn the language: Issues in theory and research. In R. M. Manchón (Ed.), *Learning-to-write and writing-to-learn in an additional language.* (pp. 61–82). Amsterdam, The Netherlands: John Benjamins.

Paltridge, B., Harbon, L., Hirsch, D., Shen, H., Stevenson, M., Phakiti, A., & Woodrow, L. (2009). *Teaching academic writing: An introduction for teachers of second language writers.* Ann Arbor, MI: University of Michigan Press.

Rinnert, C., & Kobayashi, H. (2009). Situated writing practices in foreign language settings: The role of previous experience and instruction. In R. M. Manchón (Ed.), *Writing in foreign language contexts: Learning, teaching, and research* (pp. 49–76). Bristol, England: Multilingual Matters.

Sasaki, M. (2009). Changes in EFL students' writing over 3.5 years: A socio-cognitive account. In R. M. Manchón (Ed.), *Writing in foreign language contexts: Learning, teaching, and research* (pp. 49–76). Bristol, England: Multilingual Matters.

Tardy, C. M. (2009). *Building genre knowledge*. West Lafayette, IN: Parlor Press.

Tardy, C. M., & Matsuda, P. K. (2009). The construction of author voice by editorial board members. *Written Communication, 26*, 32–52.

CHAPTER SIX

Utopian Alienation

Becoming an Academic Writer in the USA

KEN NIELSEN

INTRODUCTION

I arrived at Newark Airport on a flight from Copenhagen, Denmark. In my passport I had my coveted F1 visa. In my bag I had proof that I had been admitted to a graduate school of my dreams. Among the many reasons why I decided to attend graduate school in the United States was the dream that I would one day write a book. Or, rather, I had a fantasy of becoming a writer. Though it was yet under-articulated, writing was at the core of what I was going to become. The culminating experience of my Danish master's degree from the University of Copenhagen had been a book-length manuscript, so producing a sustained piece of writing was not completely foreign to me. However, as I was to discover, I had a lot to learn not only about writing itself but also about what being a professional writer means, and, not least, how it feels. Curiously, I had never thought about the centrality of writing to the project I had somehow got myself into. In my field, to be a PhD student is to be a writer; to be an academic is to be a writer.

This chapter is written to guide the student new to the United States in the process of becoming an academic writer. Drawing on analogies from my field, theatre, I suggest that you can benefit from thinking strategically about yourself as what I call an alienated writer who participates in a utopian community of knowledge production. I offer two brief theoretical reflections followed by four concrete strategies. These reflections see writing as performance, and encourage you to begin to "act the part" of the academic writer in a play of pronouns where writing is seen as a rehearsal.

STARTING TO BECOME A WRITER

While the transition into a doctoral program is personally and academically challenging for any student, it is even more so for the international student who is facing the daunting process of negotiating new academic codes and rules of conduct. Of all the codes that are new to the international student entering North American academia, writing might be the hardest to negotiate and most elusive to grasp. Even for international students with a high proficiency in English, learning to write in Academic English is essential.

I received the following comment from a professor in the margin of one of my third year papers: "First, investigate your pronouns carefully. There are times when 'I' seems to have special knowledge, but other times when 'we' are all the same. I'm not sure you're entirely consistent in your argument."

At the time, I understood the comment to be mechanical: figure out when to invoke yourself and when to rely on a more rhetorical and distanced "we." However, as I moved into the dissertation phase and started to struggle with the writing of it (something that came as a surprise to me, as I had always enjoyed writing and been told that I was pretty good at it), I came to think more consciously about the deeper significance of "I" and "we." Throughout my previous education, I realized, "I," as a person, had been inseparable from the writing and thinking in my papers. I was the writing, and I had never reflected on the separation of the two—*I* as a person, and *I* as a producer of academic text. However, the *I* of the writing is separable from the *I* of the person. Likewise, the universal *we* is exactly not universal but a very particular *we*: that of the academic audience, and, in particular, a North American academic audience in a specific field.

By understanding the act of writing in North American academia as something to *perform* rather than something to embody, you will be able to appreciate your own rhetorical background as something valuable while performing in a new North American register. Thinking consciously about the act of writing as performance will enable you to consider initial failures with the codes of North American academia as signs that more rehearsal is needed, rather than as personal failures or signs of some inherent lack of intellectual capability.

BRECHTIAN ALIENATION

In order to explain to you how I came to think of myself as an academic writer working in a language that was not my own, I turn to the German theatre director and theorist, Bertolt Brecht.

Bertolt Brecht—one of the great revolutionizers of 20th-century theatre—wanted to create a socially conscious theatre that did not rely on absolute identification between actor and character or on an absolute identification between spectator and character (Brecht, 1992). He wanted a theatre that pointed to its own construction, its own performativity and fictionality, and a theatre that made its audiences reflect on the social conditions presented on stage and in their own world. A central component in achieving this goal was the *Verfremdungseffekt*, or Alienation effect (Brecht, 1992, p. 193). Employing the Alienation effect, an actor would simultaneously be his own person and the character. Brecht believed an audience member would always be aware that what she saw was not King Lear as a person but simply an actor playing a character called King. In "A Short Organum for the Theatre," Brecht (1992) wrote:

> In order to produce A-effects the actor has to discard whatever means he has learnt of getting the audience to identify itself with the characters which he plays. Aiming not to put his audience into a trance, he must not go into a trance himself. (p. 193)

He continued: "Even if he plays a man possessed he must not seem to be possessed himself, for how is the spectator to discover what possessed him if he does" (Brecht, 1992, p. 193)? For the purposes of this chapter, the question is, of course, what does this have to do with becoming an academic writer?

The Brechtian dialectic here (the relationship between the person and the character) can be productive in separating the personal from the scholarly, the *writing I* from the *personal I*. In turn, it can help us point to a collective we without assuming full knowledge of that we. It can help us produce texts that are clearly material manifestations of our thought, but also texts that continuously point to themselves not as magically produced but as produced through labor. It can help us unlearn our inherited notion of "inspiration" (a belief that remains prevalent and one in which the undergraduate pulls an all-nighter and finishes a paper in a possessed state), and instead adopt a praxis.

WRITING AS A UTOPIAN PERFORMATIVE

When international students enter the North American academy, they're asked to be something that they are not yet: scholars. They're apprentices, and, as such, we can think of them as performers. They're in the process of becoming something that they're not yet. In other words, they're rehearsing. The question before us, then, is how can we think of the writing classroom as a space for performance and rehearsal, and, furthermore, what can thinking of writers and readers as actors and spectators do for us? While the ramifications of this question go beyond the scope of this short chapter, it's productive to turn briefly to feminist theatre scholar Jill Dolan's (2008) notion of the Utopian Performative.

Dolan (2008) defined the concept as,

> describe[ing] small but profound moments in which performance calls the attention of the audience in a way that lifts everyone slightly above the present, into a hopeful feeling of what the world might be like if every moment of our lives were as emotionally voluminous, aesthetically striking, and intersubjectively intense. (p. 5)

Granted, Dolan is thinking about actual performance and I'm borrowing the concept for a different framework; however, I think that Dolan's "intersubjectivity" can become the dynamic of a classroom in which writers are allowed to imagine a more utopian mastery of the academic essay than the one they currently have. This utopian imagination in turn sustains their work and progress toward greater complexity and revelry in uncertainty. If we think of writers as alienated actors (with alienated being a positive word) and the seminar room or writing group as a space in which utopian performances can happen, the apprentice writer might be able to set him or herself free to experiment, fail, try again, and succeed. Writing in graduate school is rehearsal; treat it as such.

FOUR STRATEGIES: NOW, TELL ME WHY THAT MATTERS AGAIN!

You may be thinking at this point that writing in graduate school is a nice idea, but how would this work in the real world of seminars and comprehensive exams? Rather than simply *being* writers we need to think about ourselves *becoming* writers who are able to point to our texts as products of labor. Treating our process as one of rehearsal allows for moments of utopian performatives during which we *imagine* what we can still become and what a community of thinkers and writers might feel like. Four concrete strategies can be considered for working with these ideas. They will help you think more clearly of yourself as an academic writer in a North American context: praxis, revisions, separation, and demystification.

Praxis

Writing is a praxis. Praxis is the act of transforming ideas and thought into material form and it should be treated as work.

It's important for any new graduate student to get to know the conversations of the field, but it's even more so for the international student whose national academic discussion might be quite different than the one taking place in North America. Knowing both discourses (the national and the North American discourse) is a strength, but it takes a conscious and alienated reader to keep both in mind. Reading and writing about these readings in note form will be your job for a couple of years. I personally recommend finding a library in which to do this work, every day. Get up, get dressed, go to the library, work, repeat. Allocating set hours is important for your writing and reading work. There will be time to discover the city afterwards.

Writing is a continuous process of exploration and explanation: you explore your ideas and arguments in the draft, then you explain those ideas to your reader in the revision. Remember that you cannot explain what you have not explored. When you get to the dissertation stage, you might find yourself in situations where it takes a while to get your drafts back from your readers. Disassociate yourself from the readers. Remember that the work is not you; the time it takes readers to read your work is not a judgment of you. Their schedules are full of committee meetings, conferences, and classes to teach. Remember your utopian community and the alienated writer. You can keep producing work while waiting for a chapter to be returned. You can't control the response time, but don't let it become an excuse for not moving forward. Fall back on your praxis and remember that while you have now explained a part of your dissertation to the reader, you can start enjoying the freedom in exploring the next chapter without the difficult decisions that come with revisions.

Form a writing group with people whose work interests you. Do this early on and become each other's readers. You don't have to be friends: in fact, it's sometimes easier if you're not. You should be friendly—you don't want to spend time hanging around people you don't like or whose work does not stimulate you intellectually—but that is different from being friends. Treat this writing group as a utopian rehearsal space. Think of yourself as a group of alienated writers coming together to practice your skill and profession. In this space, in glimpses, I guarantee you'll experience moments of utopian existence and radical thought.

Take your own praxis as a writer seriously. Draw on all the help that might be offered you. Your institution is sure to have a writing center of some sort (sometimes this will be under a health and wellness center). Writing centers often have a reputation for being spaces of remediation. They're not. They're utopian spaces where writers find interested and capable readers to help them further their craft and potential. Remember, the writing *I* is not your person and your writing is not a judgment of you.

Revisions

International graduate student writers will be given tons of good advice by their advisors, such as don't end a sentence with a preposition; avoid dangling modifiers; don't start a sentence with a conjunction; use the semicolon to connect closely related sentences; and, best of all: be clear. While these grammatical conventions are all great and well-meant pieces of advice, they can also be less than useful in that they hinder the writer from understanding what is really missing in the piece in order to undertake the process of radical revision.

In 1980 composition scholar Nancy Sommers published her study on the revision strategies of student writers and compared these to those of experienced adult writers. She found that the two groups had widely different understandings of what revision means. Student writers primarily understood revision as a lexical exercise—changing one word for another, refining the vocabulary, working with dictionaries and thesauruses, etc.—while more experienced writers understood revision as both a lexical and a semantic process. In other words, experienced writers thought not of revision but of revisions, of multiple iterations of their texts. As Sommers (1980) discovered: "The experienced writers see their revision process as a recursive process—a process with significant recurring activities—with different levels of attention and different agenda for each cycle" (p. 386). In other words, experienced writers understand the writing process as a recursive process during which the writer continuously discovers new aspects of her manuscript. You need to be willing to assess your argument repeatedly, ask yourself if the evidence really shows what you claim it does, and, probably only in the third or fourth round of revisions, you need to ask yourself if this or that word is the right one to use. Radical revision takes courage and is dependent on the ability to step outside of yourself and look at your text afresh. Practicing being an alienated writer will help you do this because it helps establish the necessary distance between the text and you, the writer, not you, the *I*.

Understanding the revision process as one happening primarily on the semantic level rather than the lexical level is particularly important for the international student. I remember moments in my life as a graduate student when I would finish a sentence containing words like discursively, ontologically, epistemologically (yes, in the same sentence) and be very proud of my control of this new language of mine. There was only one problem: I wasn't really in control of this language; instead, I was hiding behind sentences drawing on jargon in an effort to feel and sound smart. A more alienated writer than the one I used to be would have been able to first identify my fear of inadequacy; then separate it from the text. An alienated writer would focus on producing a text that didn't aim to impress; that focused its attention on a robust intellectual argument rather than a scholarly code that the writer thought he needed to belong in the ivory tower; and, finally, producing a text that communicated its argument in clear yet sophisticated prose. The only way for all of this to happen is through a series of radical revisions and engagements with readers (be they advisors, writing group members, or writing center consultants).

Separation

As a graduate student you're an apprentice expected to enter into a conversation that is important to your chosen discipline and field. This can be a daunting task when you are writing in a foreign language. Once you've read widely in the conversations written about these texts to explore what you think about them and how their arguments will help you develop your own ideas, you want to think about your authority as a writer. Part of this is thinking about your ethos, who you are on the page.

The international student always speaks from a multiplicity of subject positions. Everybody does, of course, but I think this is truer of international students. Taking this position seriously by being conscious of it is important in the writing process and the production of knowledge that happens on the page. Jim Corder (1985), for example, wrote that,

> Argument is partial; when a speaker argues a proposition or develops a theme or makes an assertion, he or she has knowingly or not chosen one proposition, one theme, one assertion from all available. When we speak, we stand somewhere, and our standing place makes both known and silent claims upon us. (p. 31)

Our choices, then, define us and the place from where we speak will be defined partly by these choices. One way of clarifying to the reader where you stand is to engage your sources strategically, thereby carving out space for yourself in the conversation. Being an alienated writer, you know that text is not magical, but a material production of thought. Using this awareness strategically will help you be clear and persuasive.

There are many ways to carve out space for yourself in the conversation, but one of the most productive I've found (particularly in teaching undergraduates the academic essay, though I think it's likewise productive for writers new to North American academic discourse) involves engaging the strategies developed by Mark Gaipa (2004). To Gaipa, authority "is less a characteristic than a relationship that a writer has with other authors, measuring how powerfully his or her work affect theirs" (p. 419). In other words, authority is not some dominant trait in a writer but is instead built through the careful construction of relationships between sources and writers. In his article, stick figures and all, Gaipa outlined the following strategies for working with sources: Picking a Fight, Ass Kissing, Piggybacking, Leapfrogging, Playing Peacemaker, Acting Paranoid, Dropping Out, and, Crossbreeding the Conversation with Something New. And here is another instance of where alienation and utopian performatives combine—the alienated writer already knows that as a writer she is constantly engaged in a dialectical exchange of materials that is at once part of her and a material manifestation of thought. She also realizes that when producing a motivated academic argument, she is part of the production of a larger community of thinkers: a community devoted to a production of knowledge for the betterment of the human world. Though Gaipa's (2004) strategies can be accused of being schematic (which they deliberately are), they are forceful ways for you to start thinking about how you can make space for yourself at the table of whatever scholarly conversation you're aiming to enter.

Demystification

Different educational systems value different things in written communication and intellectual argumentation. The international student brings with her a set of assumptions about what a good academic essay is and these assumptions might clash with the values of North American academia. An example: I once had a student with a French educational background in one of my writing seminars. All semester long she and I battled over her writing, which I found opaque and abstract and she found delightful and provocative. The truth is, it was all of that. She was used to writing in a French tradition that looks very little like the straight-forward nature of the North American academic essay. Only after she exploded: "but English is such a pedestrian language!" (and we had a good laugh) could we move on and think about her resistance to the format of the papers I was asking her to write.

Once she had been able to voice her resistance, she started thinking about the format as a code, a language, essentially, that she needed to master in order to succeed at the university that she was now in. She realized that I wasn't asking her to change what she valued in writing (the opaque, abstract, delightful, and provocative) but rather to take her delight and translate it into a form and language that her new readers would be familiar with. In other words, I asked her to become an alienated writer capable of imagining the utopian community that she had sought access to by the very nature of her decision to attend this particular institution in the very particular world of the North American academy.

This anecdote is illustrative in thinking about what demystifying rhetorical assumptions of what an academic argument looks like. By being conscious about the culturally specific nature of the writing you'll be asked to produce, you will write clearer essays with less frustration. This doesn't mean that you'll need to forget your own rhetorical background, but rather that you'll gain access to a new language. To that end, develop a lexicon for your own writing (or if your institution has one, familiarize yourself with it and use it). Finally, a great way to demystify your writing and process is to write cover letters for all papers and chapters you'll be submitting during coursework and the writing of your dissertation. By writing a letter in which you point out the qualities and struggles of the paper or chapter, you force yourself to alienate yourself from the paper, look at its performance, and then explain this to your reader. Here, a shared lexicon is also helpful and furthers the process of separating the *I* and the *we*.

FINALLY

I have sought to think about the implications of *I* and *we;* the alienated writer *I* and the utopian *we* with which this *I* communicates. I've proposed that it is helpful to separate the personal from the professional act of writing. Even academic writing is personal, of course, but it should not be internalized as a reflection of our inner self and personal worth. It is an expression of your thinking and should as such be separated from your sense of self: it's a product of labor. Far too often we are taught to believe that writing emerges from the soul by some sort of magical if not outright divine inspiration. This is not true. Learning how to write is a process that takes time, but being conscious about this solitary process and its connection to a utopian community of readers will make the process easier, and, I think, more productive for all. As you do so, always remember to "investigate your pronouns carefully!" Because, after all, you are not necessarily the *I* and the *you* is not necessarily the *we*.

REFERENCES

Brecht, B. (1992). A short organum for the theatre. In J. Willett (Ed.), *Brecht on theatre: The development of an aesthetic* (pp. 179–205). New York, NY: Hill & Wang.

Corder, J. W. (1985). Argument as emergence, rhetoric as love. *Rhetoric Review, 4*(1), 16–32. Retrieved from http://www.jstor.org/stable/465760

Dolan, J. (2008). *Utopia in performance: Finding hope at the theater.* Ann Arbor, MI: University of Michigan Press.

Gaipa, M. (2004). Breaking into the conversation: How students can acquire authority for their writing. *Pedagogy: Critical Approaches to Teaching Literature, Language, Composition, and Culture, 4*(3), 419–437. Retrieved from https://muse.jhu.edu/journals/pedagogy/v004/4.3gaipa.pdf

Sommers, N. (1980). Revision strategies of student writers and experienced adult writers. *College Composition and Communication, 31*(4), 378–387. Retrieved from http://www.jstor.org/stable/356588

CHAPTER SEVEN

Thinking Bigger

Editing a Book 101

CHRISTOPHER MCMASTER

INTRODUCTION

At the start of my doctoral studies I was asked by a friend, "what do you want to do with your PhD when you finish?" I thought for a moment and told him that I would like to use it to work abroad, that I would try to find work with an NGO (non-governmental organization).

My friend, Tariq, only shook his head at my answer. "Chris," he said, "you think too small. You have to learn to think bigger."

His confident rebuff to my plans of working for an NGO was simple: "You don't work for an NGO, Chris, you make your own."

Tariq was many years my junior, but that wasn't evident from looking at his resume. He had left his war-torn country to study abroad, earning a master's in the United States, and was then beginning his own PhD. He had worked for the United Nations, the United States State Department, and several international charities. To him, his PhD was a way to give back to his country, to help it heal. I admired his conviction and I listened to his words. He may not know it, but those words have shadowed my studies. They have haunted any plans I make for the future. Indeed, am I thinking big enough?

In this chapter I take my friend's advice and offer a "how to" in thinking bigger: how to edit/co-edit your own book. During your postgraduate studies you are encouraged to publish. When my supervisor first suggested that I turn some initial research into a paper for submission to a national journal I felt a bit of trepidation. However, through her encouragement I submitted additional papers as well. As I had been writing and publishing by myself for the first 2 years of my doctoral study I wondered what "collaboration" might feel like. How could I work collaboratively with fellow students to produce something that is engaging and useful for the academic community? The original ideal wasn't a book, it was simply a desire to collaborate—thinking bigger, beyond my own study. The result would eventually be an edited book written by postgraduate students for postgraduate students. It would involve 25 contributors from not just my university, but from all over the country. It involved thinking bigger, thinking past the publication of articles. I co-edited this book simultaneously with writing up my own thesis, and saw its publication 2 months prior to my viva voce. While waiting for that oral examination I took the idea to Australia, the United States, South Africa, and the United Kingdom.

Think bigger. It is a simple message, but scary and difficult at the same time. However, it is a message with merit, and pregnant with possibility. In the following sections I will take you through the process of co-editing my first book. The lessons and stages I went through in that project will undoubtedly be different in detail to projects I may pursue in future, or that you may face. The sequence, however, and the basic ingredients of that sequence, may just start a chain of thought that begins with an idea, and continues with a bit of gumption. The sequence of steps below is offered as an apprenticeship of sorts—letting you know what to expect, what to start thinking about, and when to think about it. There are, of course, some details missing in this outline. As each project is different there will be more to learn each time. In publishing this book I am repeating a formula that worked well the first time, but I am still learning. That type of learning is what makes us better at what we do.

AN ORGANIZED LEADER

The outline below is based on my own, admittedly limited, experience, but that experience contains many useful lessons. One key thing to remember is to be *organized*. Keep a wall diary and a physical folder, if that is how you work, or keep electric folders and reminders. Never let the beast run away from you. There will be hectic and busy times, so be warned. And be prepared. These times are manageable if you plan for them and are *organized*. If you like to compartmentalize, then do so: set an hour or two aside a day or week to focus solely on this project. If you like to multitask, have multiple screens open on your computer. Everybody works differently. I liked to work on multiple projects simultaneously. I found that the more I had going on the more I got done. Work the way *you* work best. BUT, to keep to a schedule, to get others to work to your standard and your timeline, and to keep their confidence in you as editor: be *organized*.

Editing a book is also all about leadership, and being a good leader. Much of good leadership is good people-managing and people skills. You will be juggling many different personalities—what makes them similar is the result: you want a good chapter for your book. You are all working toward the same goal, which is a successfully edited book. There may be times when you are direct, but being direct is not the same as being tactless or discourteous. There may be times when you have to bite your tongue. During those times, swallow the blood and smile through it. When you have to be a "dick," manage it professionally. There was a situation with one contributor that I had to cut from a book. She was a well-established academic and offered a well-written chapter, but it just did not fit the tone and flow of the rest of the book. The way I managed this was to give that contributor an out—I let her make the decision to take her chapter elsewhere, even if it "appeared" that I had backed down. Ego is important, but needs to be managed as well. For me, in that situation, it was more important that every party felt their sense of honor, or self-worth, was intact. That was much more important to me and my project than an egotistical need to feel in control or dominant. People skills are important. It is all very political, in the sense of how you relate to others.

Ultimately, the message is to stay on top of the work as well as all the relationships involved. This type of project is based on relationships, after all, and involves a good deal of work. This work will occur in a sequential manner that I attempt to outline below. These steps include what you may have to do, perhaps should do, what you should expect, what you should be prepared for.

GETTING STARTED

Establish a good team to co-edit with, and learn each person's strengths—what they can bring to the project. This will be very important in establishing expectations and dividing up workloads. I know I am good with concepts and content, as in flow and consistency of voice. I am not so good at copy editing or recognising some mistakes in text. So it was important for me to find somebody good at that and to be able to step aside and let them work their kind of magic. I may also have been a type of captain that encouraged mutiny or disaster in a past life, like Ahab chasing his white whale. Having somebody on the team that can keep that kind of ego in check is important. This is all about being honest about your strengths and weaknesses. There was a time in my first book, for a whole day, where I was the sole editor. My original co-editor was unable to continue and I was faced with completing the project on my own. But being honest with myself during that sleepless night, I realised that if I had a co-editor who compensated for my weaknesses, the book would not just be "good," but "outstanding." A phone call the next day established a partnership that is still strong.

As you begin your project, set up an e-mail account that can be used as a communication hub for contributors and can be accessed by co-editors. While you manage the site and communications, it is good to share access—your co-editors may be able to communicate more effectively with some contributors, as their proposed abstracts may be more closely aligned with their areas of experience or expertise. The sharing of access and communication will also build cohesion among the team. Gmail is an example of an application that can be useful for this purpose, although your co-editors will need Gmail accounts to be able to have access. These are easy to set up. Skype allows you to hold conference calls, which will be vital for key shared decisions. Cloud storage such as Dropbox allows for team access to documents. Good communication also enables you to exercise good leadership. I always interpret "good leadership" as one that isn't based on a single personality. If you communicate openly with your team, then should you be incapacitated, for whatever reason, the project will continue to advance.

Once you have an idea for a potential book, draft a very good call for abstracts. Send this to your team members so that they can have input. It is amazing how much better some documents read after they have been co-written or co-edited. Your call for abstracts will concisely describe to potential contributors what your book is all about. Spend the time describing this clearly. This work will be invaluable when you are "selling" the book to a publisher, as well as drafting the blurb that will be on the back cover. Before I completed my first call for abstracts I sent the idea as a concept to an established academic I trusted, asking, "What do you think of this idea?" That e-mail assuaged my own (at the time) weak confidence, and that kind of reassurance can be offered by your academic mentors.

With your call for abstracts, create a timeline for the project and stick to it as far as possible. Let your team know and agree with this. How long do you want to give to collect abstracts? More time means more opportunity to reach potential contributors. Too much time may mean losing momentum. Consider the balance, and figure into the timeline you and your co-editor's other responsibilities. If you are writing a thesis or lecturing, don't have chapters coming for review during a crucial time, such as marking assignments or preparing a chapter or a conference presentation. Create a schedule that suits your team. Drive the process consciously.

When you are happy with the call for abstracts, send it as far and wide as possible. Use all your contacts, be clever and think of the most efficient way to send out the call. In the Australian version of this book, this was through what was known as the Thesis Whisperer. That avenue alone reached hundreds, even thousands, of potential contributors. After that we utilized individual contacts at different universities. And, just because you send a call to a specific department or school, that does not mean it will go to other parts of the university. How will you ensure your call goes elsewhere? In the United States, a few hours were spent contacting graduate associations at individual universities. As we were trying to reach graduate students and potential contributors, going to the source seemed more logical than going through their deans.

Be clever. You are not only sending out a call for abstracts, but also making contacts and networking. If you want to work in tertiary education, contacting established scholars is also a way to say, "Look at me, you may want to hire me if I apply for a job at your institution."

AN ORGANIZED PROFESSIONAL

Be very organized when abstracts for your book come in. Abstracts will come in for the length of time that you specify in your call. Some will come sooner, some will come later. Create a folder where you keep these. Number each abstract and give it a clear title. Create a separate document where you list in table form each abstract topic and author, with each author's e-mail. The number on this table should correspond with the numbered file in the abstract folder. When your team looks at all the abstracts and decides what is in and what is not, you want that to be as easy for you and them as possible. This folder could be openly accessed by your team throughout the collection process through a shared Dropbox account or Google Docs. If this is how your team prefers to work then the ultimate selection process may be quite straightforward as you will all be very familiar with the proposed chapters.

Use the submission process to also communicate with potential contributors. What may seem a "quiet" period in the project can actually be very interesting. As potential contributors ask you about the project you grow in confidence and clarity as to what your project is. You can ask them to alter their abstract to more suit your book concept, or to answer any of their questions. This is an important time to build relationships with potential contributors but also to make it clear what you want from potential contributors. During this time even more concept ideas for projects may present themselves. While collecting abstracts for the Australian version of this book several people wrote from farther afield asking why the idea was so geographically limited. From those e-mails came a United Kingdom and a United States version. Thinking bigger sometimes has a tendency to lead to even bigger things.

During the entire process, remember: act, and be, professional, or how you define "professional." You are the "expert" and the trusted leader in this venture. Contributors will expect this. They will not want to be a part of a project that appears weak or ad hoc. Ooze confidence, even if you don't feel it. Saying that, be realistic about your confidence and don't make empty promises. In the initial stages of the first postgraduate book I fielded several questions about a publisher for the book. I understood this concern—why should somebody invest their time in my project if there is no guarantee of a result? My belief in the project was, however, contagious. "Find a publisher?" I confidently responded, "Of course we will, this project will sell itself." The caveat to confident responses is that they must be based on reality. Being confident means believing in yourself and your project, and never lying or "stringing people along."

BUILDING A BOOK

When the period of accepting abstracts has elapsed, with your co-editors sort out the abstracts you want with your co-editors. Use those abstracts to create a detailed outline of the book. Your decisions will create a table of contents. Publishers appreciate that—you will be giving them a blueprint when you submit a proposal, not a concept. You will also be demonstrating to any prospective publisher that you are organized and serious—that you can deliver what they require, when they require it.

After the decision to accept abstracts, e-mail all those accepted and provide them with writing guidelines and a timeline. Writing guidelines re-iterate the purpose of the book and give the contributors an idea of the type of tone and content you desire. This is a very important document so draft it well. The clearer you are, even in formatting their chapters, the smoother the process of editing their chapters will be. What you are expecting from your contributors are well-written and well-drafted chapters, so encourage them to write and proof well.

In the acceptance e-mail tell them when you are submitting a proposal to a publisher. You don't have to say to whom; I didn't do that with the New Zealand (NZ) volume as I didn't want any contributors contacting the publisher, and I wanted to play it safe in case a contributor had a personal connection of some sorts with the publisher. During this period, encourage contributors to start writing and not wait for the formal book deal. Some will want to wait, that's fair enough and up to them. Tell your contributors when you have the acceptance from a publisher in a good news, "full speed ahead" e-mail to all.

Create two e-mail lists: one list with names and e-mail addresses, the other with all the contributor e-mails, which can be cut and pasted onto the "send to" bar. Or you can be clever and have your group e-mail already set up. I found that by having a list on a separate document I could manage the list easily when e-mails changed. Also, e-mail all those you don't choose for inclusion in your book. Be very professional and courteous. You never know when you will be working with them in future. In my "rejection" e-mails I encourage those individuals to write up their concept and seek to have it published elsewhere, or even to develop their idea into a book in its own right.

Once you have your contributors and chapter topics, create a list that you can use when you need to contact them or require a response. This can act as a tick list, a way to keep track of who has responded, given you what you needed, etc. To replay that record, it is all about being organized.

As you start to see the shape of your book, when abstracts are coming in begin searching for the publisher that would best suit your book. Investigate other titles by them—you can do this by surfing their web page. When you find the publisher you think is a great fit, contact them and say you have a great idea for a submission. Ask what the process for submission of a proposal is at their publishing company. Their website might provide that template, but contacting them also acts to introduce you to them, and you get a name to respond to. As the project progresses, the relationship between you and the publisher will be very important.

Work diligently in producing a very good book proposal. If the publisher does not have a proposal guide or framework, try borrowing one from elsewhere so you are sure all bases are covered. It is like a job application—you have to do it well if you want to be considered.

PRODUCING A BOOK

There will come a time when you have your publisher and your contributors are writing. All you may hear at this time is a clock ticking, but you have your pre-agreed timeline to follow. Send out a reminder before the first deadline (chapter drafts). You will hopefully get a few chapters before the deadline date.

When the deadline is reached you will be busy. Will every chapter cross your desk? That means that every chapter returned by a contributor will be personally read and edited by you. I had to do that in the NZ volume as I didn't have help at that stage. It was a great process, and allowed me total control of the tone of the book (I've already confessed my "Ahab" tendencies earlier in the chapter), but it was also a great deal of work. I track-marked and commented throughout each chapter and sent them back to the contributors to keep working on them. Some were very well written; others needed a great deal of attention. While it enabled me to ensure a consistent voice in the book, to make sure all the contributors wrote the way I wanted (in their own voice, of course), it taught me balance. My primary priority at this time was writing up my own thesis!

During this time, share this work among your co-editors. If your book has sections, perhaps you can take charge of different sections. I actually think this makes for a better book—it lets each co-editor focus on a section and make it really good, and builds a "section team" between each co-editor and their contributors.

QUALITY CONTROL

How will you check your own work? What kind of secondary review will you have? Each chapter will have passed by the desk of the editors, each chapter will have had feedback, may even have passed by the desk of an editor several times. There still remains an issue of quality control. Who will review the reviewers? One possibility is a section swap among co-editors. Each co-editor can swap sections and review the work presented. In the New Zealand volume we organized the contributors into pairs and swapped chapters. This worked well in some cases—some were experienced at the process, but some were novice and the process was not so robust. You could even ask if there are any contributors who would like to act as reviewers, and give them some guidelines.

When you are ready, put the chapters together into a whole book format, with a table of contents. Send the draft to whoever will be writing the foreword once the editing team is in agreement it is ready to go. Give this person a few weeks to write it. That should be built into your timeline, and they can be writing that while you are tidying up any loose ends. Choose the person to write your foreword wisely. You will have your reasons for that choice, at least you should have your reasons, whether that be your own career advancement, product placement, or honoring a friend and colleague.

When you have all the chapters and foreword, write a preface and back-of-book blurb. Include your co-editors in co-editing and co-writing. This is a group effort.

At the same time, e-mail contributors to ask for 75-word bios in third-person (for an "about the authors" section). Anywhere in the 50–100 word range is considered acceptable.

Then copyedit. Print the book off in whole, and use only a red pen. If you have ever copyedited an entire book you will understand this advice: Work with your co-editors to share the work. Type the edits into chapters (using tracking/commenting) and return the chapters to contributors to fix and consider all the edits. This is tedious work, so manage it well. It is also vitally important work. I discovered this was practice for editing my own thesis when the time came—word by word and line by line. If it is possible and you live near your co-editors (in our electronic age this is not necessary) then make an event of it. It might be hard work, but that is no reason not to enjoy it.

SENDING THE BOOK AWAY

When is a book ready to submit to a publisher? Publishers have a copy editor who will be extremely thorough, but it eases the process if they are given something you are happy with. I think my first publisher really liked working with my team.

I visited him in his office during a trip to "the city" and enjoyed a nice chat. I looked at his white board, his "to do" list regarding the many projects he oversaw, and I asked him, "We are an easy one for you, aren't we?" By being organized, and by being robust regarding your quality, you will be an "easy one" for the publisher. That can be interpreted as being someone they may be happy working with again.

What details might be missing, as at this stage you will be considering details? Cover art? Now may be the time to use any contacts with artists. If your book is by and for graduate students with disabilities, as an example, then why not have cover art representing that audience, by that audience? The publisher will appreciate you doing this kind of work, but be aware that they know how to make a book and have the final say about how things will go together.

Maintain good communication with contributors during this time. Communication is a balancing act—keeping momentum and enthusiasm. I wrote a chapter for a book during my first year of study and heard from the editors twice in 2 years. I still don't know when that book will be out. I didn't want to be that kind of editor on my own project. It doesn't take much effort to send an e-mail to all your contributors to let them know where things are at.

And during this time, while the book is out of your hands and in those of the real pros, keep sweet with the publisher, but maintain the integrity of your project. Major issues may not arise, and be prepared to be flexible, but be an advocate for your contributors and your book.

FINAL THOUGHTS

Reading through my words I can't help but think about all the details that may not have made it to text, or all the situations that might arise for you, that I haven't mentioned. What I have presented is a possibility, as well as a challenge. Think bigger. I was hesitant when my friend Tariq first asked about my plans, and I also tried to explain to him why such a question was difficult to answer. I knew that there were doors that might open that I could not even see during those early days of my study; doors that I didn't even know existed. While I had notions of what I might do with my qualification, I was going to keep an open mind to what might present itself. I think it is just as important to keep an open mind as to what you might be able to accomplish during your studies. Like publish a book.

CHAPTER EIGHT

Paying It Forward

Engaging the Next Generation of Professional Students

DANIELLE SHEPHERD

INTRODUCTION

You will encounter unique experiences as a graduate student, but some aspects of graduate school will be similar for us all. We will each have an advisor, some type of research to perform, a dissertation to write and defend, and a committee that will decide whether we graduate. As a graduate student, you have an incredible opportunity, even responsibility, to become an inspiring educator or mentor while you are studying and researching. The distinct decision you make to inspire the next generation and the initiative you take to get involved in opportunities beyond your studies are duties that need to be fulfilled as you learn to "pay it forward" throughout graduate school.

In this chapter, I will emphasize the importance of interacting with the next generation of students, provide you with advice on how to take your first step toward reaching out, and demonstrate the important role you could play in this endeavor. I will share with you how I was inspired to choose a professional degree in science and how I am able to pay it forward and influence younger students through my involvement within local schools and the surrounding community. Inspiring the next generation is all about learning your unique story, how you can pay it forward, and actually getting out there to make a difference.

The primary and secondary education system is full of inspiring educators with a passion to teach students in each realm of their curriculum. I find myself pondering how great it is when current graduate students supplement what these younger students are already learning from their teachers. I am always inspired when I see the "aha moment" of a student who just made the connection on how something works or the graduate student who cannot help but smile because of the excitement of all the kids learning from what they demonstrated. Younger students look up to older students for further inspiration to follow what they love to do in school and to turn that love into a career.

When I was a young student attending a summer program called "College for Kids," I was able to select a variety of exciting classes, from fencing to astronomy and everything in between. The teachers for these classes were mostly graduate students pursuing degrees in many diverse fields. I remember going to a neuroscience class and being amazed at just how much fun science was. This graduate student made learning about synapses and the way each part of the brain communicates with the other parts fun and hands-on. This experience drastically affected my love and curiosity for science because I always enjoyed and looked forward to attending class to learn something new. Recognizing the impact that graduate students and teachers can have on young students has made all the difference for me during my graduate career to find fun, interactive ways to influence the next generation of students. In this chapter, you will gain insight and practical ideas of how you can pay it forward and inspire the next generation.

LEARN YOUR UNIQUE STORY

To begin paying it forward, learn the unique story that got you to where you are now. How did you get to graduate school? Do you remember having an outstanding teacher that inspired your love for the subject he or she was teaching? Do you remember looking up to older students thinking they knew so much about everything and that they were the coolest people you had ever met? You may have a story similar to mine where you can name an individual or a few individuals who really influenced your educational trajectory. Now that I am in graduate school, I realize that as graduate students we can easily get bogged down in our research endeavors, trying daily to repeat experiments that once yielded the results we wanted, or finding the one source that will lead us in the right direction. We spend countless hours studying and writing—writing manuscripts for publication, grants to obtain funding, and let's not forget the all-important dissertation that finalizes the completion of our graduate studies. We also spend a lot of time completing coursework that is required for us to graduate and attending seminars to further our understanding of particular topics that teach us about the innovative developments within our area of expertise. All of these requirements capture so much of our focus during our graduate career and are oftentimes the topics we spend the most time worrying about due to their importance in leading us to meet our educational goals.

Yet, with all the demands on our time and energy as graduate students, I found myself asking a very core question: Are these the things that inspired me to attend graduate school in the first place? To learn my story, I had to step back and consider what truly motivated me to attend graduate school. First, I thought it was because I wanted to do research to impact how we treat the multitude of diseases currently affecting our society. I loved science growing up and I wanted to continue on that trajectory. Now that I am almost done with my graduate education, the focus for my career goals has drastically changed. What has not changed is the unique story of how I got to graduate school, and how my graduate school experiences created a sense of the responsibility I have to inspire the next generation of students.

Think about what truly motivated you to pursue a graduate education and try to focus on that to learn your unique story. What we do in graduate school could make all of the difference in a younger student's life, not to mention change your outlook on your career goals. My inspiration to pursue a professional degree came from the individuals who invested their time into feeding my curiosity and helping me believe that I could achieve anything as long as I put my mind toward my goals and never gave up. As a middle school student, I can remember having one of the best life sciences teachers in the world. I recall that when she taught us about the different organelles and their functions within the cell, she assigned each of us a particular organelle and told us to figure out a way to physically act out the function and pretend we were the organelle. As a class, we created an entire cell and learned quickly and effectively how each organelle completed its specific function, while also having fun. Having great science teachers drastically influenced me, but the graduate students who volunteered to invest their time in me played an insurmountable role in shaping me into the scientist that I am today. Without their encouragement and willingness to get involved in teaching at "College for Kids," I would not have been introduced to the diverse science, technology, engineering, math, art, health, and fitness classes as a young student. When I think about these experiences, my interactions with the coolest teachers during this "college" experience set me on a path to always do something that I love, which turned out to be science.

Choosing to obtain my graduate degree is directly related to the teachers that captivated my attention while I was in their classes and the older students that helped me realize I could follow my dreams and do something that I loved for the rest of my life. These individuals had the ability to make science interesting and exciting. They encouraged me to explore beyond the classroom and to always ask "Why?" Sure, other circumstances also paved the way to my graduate career, but reflecting back on the internal reasons for this important decision returns me to my experiences as a young student and the willingness of the graduate students to get out and invest in the next generation. Take some time to sit down and think about your unique story that led you to where you are now.

LEAVE AN IMPACT

As you begin your journey in graduate school, think about what the world will be like if, as a society, we do not continue to invest in the next generation by encouraging them to pursue a professional degree. If we do not take hold of outreach opportunities in our community as graduate students, or even create those outreach programs ourselves, we may miss our chance to influence the next generation of biomedical scientists, archaeologists, historians, business executives, social activists. You might come to find, as I did, that children in schools near your university are unaware of opportunities in graduate education due to a lack of resources. Students may be uninterested in the fields that we work in because we have neglected to ignite their interest. Graduate students can enter this situation and make an impact.

Opportunities to interact with young students may not be readily available to you through your graduate program, as I experienced during my graduate career. After networking with teachers in the community, I found that they were more than willing to open up their classrooms for graduate students to come and engage their students. Diverse avenues exist for you to get involved; you just have to look for them. No matter what field of study you are pursuing, you can leave an impact on younger students just by taking the time to sit and talk with them about what you do. If I had only known how much of a difference a couple of hours can mean to a young student, then I would have become involved in outreach earlier in my graduate career. I would have frequently offered to be a judge at science fairs, host science days in schools, and teach undergraduate courses, not just because I love science, but to be an example to both the students I taught and my graduate colleagues. I would have better utilized my career as a graduate student to show younger students the opportunities provided through education, making a career doing what you love, and how they can make a positive difference. The excitement from young students about learning is contagious, and even though we go to teach them something, we also learn from them that we should be excited about what we do, further reminding us of why we chose to pursue a graduate career. If someone asked you the purpose and practical use of an advanced degree, what would you answer? I would be willing to bet that in some capacity it would involve leaving an impact on someone or advancing your particular field. So now the question is, *how* can we as graduate students actually make a difference?

MAKE A DIFFERENCE

To make a difference, all you have to do is get out there and talk with people. While you may want to make a difference, if there is not an avenue for you to get out and interact with the community or young students, it may be a difficult task to accomplish.

When I enrolled as a student in a biomedical sciences doctoral program, I had to make a choice between seven different fields of science depending on where my research interests took me. As I continued through my degree program, met deadlines, and finished coursework, I realized that some part of my graduate career felt empty. I wanted to make an impact while I was in graduate school and I was not sure how to make that happen. Unfortunately, our program did not facilitate a way to get into the local schools and interact with the community. After some time, the Graduate Student Organization was reinstated for the biomedical sciences program and one of our goals was to increase outreach opportunities for graduate students, particularly scientific outreach.

After our first year as a new organization, we decided that it was essential to get involved with local elementary, middle, and high schools. As graduate students, we wanted to make a difference and leave an impact on younger students, so we needed to generate an avenue through the organization to accomplish this goal. We focused our efforts on programs hosted by the local children's discovery museum and any other event with which we could help. This was not as easy of a task as we thought it would be, and it took us another year to establish connections that generated outreach opportunities for our graduate students. Once we established a few connections, it was easy to be a part of annual events, but it was still a challenge to get into the school system without knowing anyone that worked there. We were unsure of how we could help or what we could do for activities, but we were determined to make this happen. We utilized a number of paths to get into the local schools and do scientific outreach with the students. One such avenue was teaming up with the undergraduate neuroscience organization and working with them at events such as Numbers and Neuroscience Night and Brain Day. We also started to reach out to principals at different schools who were able to put us in contact with individuals who held optional school-wide events, such as science fairs and STEM nights. We started utilizing the connections we had with individual teachers, who were more than happy to host a science day at their school or allow us to come into their classroom for an afternoon. Once we began employing our networking connections, we were asked to be judges at regional science bowls and state-wide science fairs because of our organization's diverse areas of expertise in the sciences.

There is an overwhelming need for individuals with a passion in a particular discipline to step out of their comfort zones and dive into the opportunities when they present themselves. You never know if you will inspire the next Wright brother or Thomas Edison. Get out there and get involved. If your program does not currently have a mechanism or venue for you to get involved in some type of outreach, that's OK, mine didn't either. Even though we struggled as an organization to pave the way for scientific outreach, most universities actually employ individuals to make the needed relationships between the university and the community, whether in schools or in companies. For example, if you are getting your professional degree in biomedical sciences, there may not be someone in the biomedical sciences program who does community education and outreach as their job; however, if you go down to the chemistry department, they may have a group of individuals who are instrumental in fortifying connections to impact the community. Look for the opportunities and be open to getting outside of your field in order to get your foot in the door and be an influential graduate student in local outreach. If you try this route and still don't have any luck, you can try what our Graduate Student Organization did to make scientific education and outreach a goal by creating an entire committee devoted to finding events in which we could participate.

When trying to get involved in community outreach within your specific program, you have to be adaptable and take advantage of the opportunities that are thrown at you. When you want to leave an impact or make a difference, you need to have a go-getter attitude and be ready to jump over obstacles that come your way. Most of the time in graduate school, the things you work the hardest for are those of which you are most proud. Outreach works the same way. You may struggle interacting with students in the beginning, but if you work through it, you will become a better communicator and add a new and refined skill to your professional tool belt. On the other hand, outreach may be something that is easy for you and opportunities may abound at your institution. If that is you, I commend you and your institution because you are already leaving an impact on your community and young students, along with setting an example for graduate students around you.

CONCLUSION

At the start of my doctoral studies, I did not fully understand the impact I could have on younger students. Reflecting on my own "unique story" enabled me to remember my time as a student who looked up to my teachers, graduate students, and other individuals who took the time to encourage me to pursue my dreams in science. Reflecting on my story allowed me to recognize the impact I have potentially made in young students' lives during my graduate career. In most universities, there is no requirement to get outside of the classroom and engage with students in a manner to promote your field of study. In fact, some of your advisors may encourage you to do nothing besides attending classes and seminars and spending every extra moment working to complete your degree. The experiences you have during your graduate career are up to you, and I am a witness to the fact, from the perspective of both a student and a teacher, that you can have an enormous impact on the lives of many young students.

You may have an uphill battle to find an area where you can give back and impact the next crop of scientists, historians, educators, or statisticians, but learning where you fit in and how you can contribute to the expansion of your field could be the legacy you want to leave at your institution. By having the willingness to move beyond my comfort zone and interact with young students interested in science and math, I have actually found further direction for my career. I want my career to be centered on shaping the minds of students and feeding their curiosity to discover new ways of thinking. My goal is to work in scientific education and outreach, which encompasses science, technology, engineering, and math, and because of the unique outreach events I have taken part in throughout graduate school, I have established connections that will make this transition into a career easier.

Graduate school is a time to discover new things about yourself, while also growing and developing in many diverse areas. Experiencing different things might give you a perspective for your field of study that you had never considered. I can guarantee that you will learn something by taking the time to interact with the next generation. You may learn that you are an excellent teacher and have a niche for communicating with children or that you are not very good at explaining all of the technical details to someone outside of your field. As a graduate student, you have the ability to learn from each of your experiences, whether it be that you are great at something that was never on your radar, or perhaps that you need to practice speaking to the lay public without using technical jargon. No matter what field of study you find yourself in, you can make a positive difference for the next generation. You will leave an impact by your willingness to make the most of opportunities that arise during your graduate career and by getting involved and interacting with the next generation of upcoming students. You never know who you will influence or what one interaction may do to spark the interest of a young student. As graduate students, it is our responsibility to help shape those who are coming into our fields after us. Get out there and make a difference.

PART THREE

Understanding
and Navigating Difference

CHAPTER NINE

We're Not in the Barrio Anymore

Negotiating Chicana/o Guilt in the Ivory Tower

RAISA ALVARADO UCHIMA Y JAIME GUZMÁN

ESTIMADA/O ESTUDIANTE

We are first generation Chicana/os born and raised in Southern California. We come from low-income families, and are the first in our families to attain both bachelor's degrees, masters degrees, and are now pursuing doctoral degrees. While our racial and cultural experiences are closely aligned, it is important for us to also acknowledge that our backgrounds, in many respects, are distinct, and informed by our unique positionalities. My familial, communal, and educational experiences as a self-identified Chicana woman are distinct from Jaime's experiences as a self-identified Chicano man. It is important for us that you know it is through our similarities and differences that we explore Chicana/o guilt in the academy. We do not claim that our experiences represent all Chicanas/os, but we offer our stories as glimpses into larger systemic obstacles present for under-represented bodies in higher education. In an effort to guide and provide authorial support, which you too may draw from, we feel it is important to briefly review our chosen methodology for this chapter. The authors we draw from have largely influenced our academic work and are sources of inspiration that empower our vision.

Performative autoethnography (Calafell & Moreman, 2010; Delgado, 2009; Griffin, 2012) as a method provides an avenue through which the marginalized-bodied can speak back to systems of power and authentically represent their lived experiences through personal narrative. Our use of performance autoethnography enables us to share our subjective experiences as brown doctoral students in a predominantly White, private university in the West, and allows us to speak to larger institutional and systemic influences affecting Chicana/o bodies. Although our accounts are our own, these individual experiences undoubtedly speak to unresolved tensions for Mexican American students in the academy. Our stories should not be homogenized as a people's story but as distinct narratives that enter into larger discussions about how brown bodies negotiate the academy. The guilt we interrogate is twofold: first, we examine the guilt associated with the literal and figural separation between us and our family and community; second, we focus on the guilt associated with "belonging" and "not belong" tension(s) (Urrieta, 2005). Finally, we sign off with survivor tips for Chicanas/os new to higher education. We now speak directly to you, future colleagues and friends. This is our story, our individual/collective struggles, our encouragement—nuestra confeción (Amaya, 2007).

CONFESIÓN(ES) I: SEPARATIONS

J: "Goodbyes" are hard to say. Especially to those you love most. The trunk of my car was packed with clothes, books, and a cobija. *Ten weeks. It will only be 10 weeks and I will be back.* Moments later, the Los Angeles skyline was in my rearview mirror and the U.S. Southwest became my landscape on my way to a different state to earn a (piece of paper) doctorate degree. As a Mexican American, I was raised with two different cultural values—*I am of Mexican decent but I am an American citizen.* As Anzaldúa (1999) argued

> *Nosotros los* Chicanos straddle the borderlands. On one side of us, we are constantly exposed to the Spanish of the Mexicans, on the other side we hear the Anglos' incessant clamoring so that we forget our language….Neither eagle nor serpent, but both. (p. 84)

Yet, as the first-born male, it has always been inscribed in my upbringing that I should take care of the family when I am old enough. *When is "old enough" and when will I know?* My decision to go to a doctorate program away from the family provides me with a daily dose of familial guilt. I should be home right now, yet I am living on my own working on a degree that will further my individual aspirations. On the surface, my actions make it seem as if I am valuing my American identity over my Mexican identity. Yet, it is a performance that hides the internal tensions Chicanas/os negotiate every day. I know that apart from missing me, my family is doing just fine back home—and yet I cannot seem to accept the fact that I decided to go to a different state to do something for *my* future. Through this personal endeavor, I am also told (in)directly that this doctorate is not just for me but for the future of the family. For a Chicano, nothing you ever do is exclusively *yours.*

"By 2002 a Pew Foundation study reported that 1.7 million Latinas/os were enrolled in US higher education institutions, though only 13 percent were in postgraduate or professional programs (Fry)" (Delgado, 2009, p. 149).

R: Chorizo, carne asada, chile, tortillas, and Coronas, the final cena embodied the best of summer. We sat around the house laughing, reminiscing, familia asking for the hundredth time about my route. Everyone had to be strong. *Si mi papá y mamá could immigrate to the United States knowing little to no English, I could do this.* It is a divisive thing, to feel your American side tugging, encouraging your personal and individual goals and to simultaneously feel your Mexican raizes. To straddle the hyphen in Mexican-American and not be able to claim sole allegiance to either,

"An American to Mexicans a Mexican to Americans, a handy token, sliding back and forth, between the fringes of both worlds" (Mora, 1984, p. 52).

I fight myself, understanding the significance of pursuing this individual academic goal, of putting my familial, marital, and *expected* maternal roles on hold for the selfish pursuit of higher education. Anzaldúa's (1999) words a resounding reminder, "In [Chicana] culture, selfishness is condemned, especially in women; humility and selflessness, the absence of selfishness, is considered a virtue" (p. 40). To be a doctoral student is to wear my selfishness like a clunky and colorful headdress. "You're doing this for them, you have to follow your dreams, you're doing this to eventually provide for *them*," White colleagues and friends remind me, assure me, without understanding. I may be in similar academic spaces but "lo mexicano is in my system" (p. 43). Anzaldúa understands, "I am a turtle, wherever I go I carry 'home' on my back" (p. 43). I feel guilt for taking care of me. *I always feel guilt.*

In 2004 "self-identified [Latina/o] faculty comprised a mere 3.38% of the total number of faculty members in the United States" (Urrieta & Chávez, 2009, p. 222).

J: 1,017 miles. I am 1,017 miles away from *mi hogar.* Leaving familiar smells, sounds, and faces to go to a state I have never visited much less ever wanted to live in. Passing two state lines, the literal separation dawns on me; my choice is extreme. Even if I wanted to, I could not get in my car and pay my family a visit within a day. Even if I wanted to, I could not afford a plane ticket home for a weekend visit. Even if I wanted to, my family would simply be *too* far away for me to have them by my side. A Mexican family is a close-knit family. *Siempre estamos juntos.* 1,017 miles. I want to blame my separation from my family on the location of the institution but this is a fruitless endeavor. When I was working on my MA degree, the institution was 5 miles away from home. School was geographically close yet the vocabulary I learned through my education was pulling me away from my family. The 5-mile commute did nothing compared to the 16 years of American institutional education. Now, more than ever, I struggle to talk to my familia. *¡Estudia* *comunicaciones y ni habla!* If they only knew that, more than anything, I wish I still knew how to talk to them. Graduate school can be so alienating.

"In 2006, specific to Mexican Americans, 8% of the population earned Bachelor's degrees, 2% earned Graduate or Professional degrees, and only. 2% of the population earned doctorate degrees" (Yosso & Solórzano, 2006).

CONFESIÓN(ES) II: PLAY THE GAME O SER BENDIDO

"In Latina/o, Chicana/o communities, the bendido/a sell-out is someone who has betrayed his or her loyalties to a group or cause" (Urrieta, 2005, p. 173).

R: My education, like that of most students of color, was predicated on two types of learning, academic and performative. Learn to add, subtract, form a cohesive thesis statement, and how to erase/hide markers of "otherness." Don't speak with a *ghetto* accent, don't wear things that show your working class status, and always bring your lunch in a brown paper bag. From an early age, social and academic experiences ingrained the need to assimilate to U.S. American culture, to perform Whiteness. I couldn't hide my prieta skin or Mexican features but I could erase my bilingual accent, withhold Spanish expressions, and eat the same food as my peers. This violent acculturation process is not uncommon for students of color who lack positive, self-affirming representations. No one in my textbooks looked like me, rarely did I encounter authority figures that spoke like me, *shit*, even on television the only time I saw myself semi-positively represented was as an over-sexed sidekick. Yet, despite these alienating experiences I survived the educational pipeline…*continue to survive.* Estimado estudiante, I would be lying if I told you these performances end. That we can comfortably and unapologetically be ourselves, and while yes, the academy can be a liberating space, it can also be a hostile and exclusionary one. One must come to terms with an academic environment they deserve to be in, earned the right to be in, and yet are not always welcomed in. To survive in these spaces is to "play the game," to pick your battles and fiercely protect yourself, but doing so comes with a cost (Urrieta, 2005). I play the game and wonder…*am I selling out?*

J: When I entered grad school in 2012, I made a political statement to correctly spell my name on papers, conference submissions, e-mail signatures, and business cards. *Was this because I wanted to pay respects to my father? Was I reclaiming the culture I rejected many years ago? Or was it because I wanted to sell my culture in order to get more traction in White academic spaces?* Yes, I am a brown body in a predominantly White institution and White discipline but what makes this even more jarring is the fact that most of my research deals with race issues. Brown bodies learn about the prevalence of race and racism well before we have those terms in our vernacular. I constantly feel that my work is delegitimized because

I am a brown person doing work on race (Calafell & Moreman, 2009). As I put words on paper, I am constantly reminded of the children in my community, most of whom will likely end up following the public school-to-prison pipeline, and that reminder sets a hard-pressed reality I can't shake off that easily because pain is never easily forgotten (like the ways in which education has made me hate my culture so much to the point of neglecting to speak Spanish for a huge part of my life). While I no longer hate my hybridized U.S. American identity, this "hate" has morphed into the impostor syndrome (Solórzano & Yosso, 2010). The constant fear that sooner rather than later my colleagues, mentors, and professors will realize that I am a fraud. At times I feel like I am unworthy of being a fully funded student in a doctoral program.

R: I'm attending a private university, a space of affluence and "prestige." A space where the student population is overwhelmingly White-with-money, a space where familial and ancestral ties grant students security, a back-up. I don't have a back-up plan. The limited resources my family has are tied up in monthly survival. This distinction is important when considering how I choose to negotiate academic spaces. Every conflict or disagreement, every opportunity to speak back to oppressive or racist statements is putting me at risk. I'm aware of how lightly I have to tread, how selective I have to be about when to speak up and when to walk away; to negotiate personal survival with speaking up. To speak to my students about power and privilege, being all too aware that I will likely be reduced to "the angry brown woman." It's a complicated tension. Every time I give in, or remain quiet, or walk away, I feel like a *sell-out*. Yet conversely, in those instances I do choose to speak back, I often leave the situation feeling drained and defeated. Guilt marks most of my decisions in these spaces. I've yet to encounter a guide for when either course of action is acceptable but I am learning to be kind to myself in a way that I did not expect. Maybe it's okay that I don't have everything figured out, and maybe…this guilt isn't always such a burden. It's a constant reminder that I am bigger than myself and that I feel empathy for other people.

EXTENDIENDO LA MANO

Graduate school is difficult, but for students of color and students who occupy marginalized identities, the experience is also alienating in profound and complicated ways. Yet, we are surviving; however, this continued survival is plagued with *survivor's guilt* (Solórzano & Yosso, 2010). We are all too aware of our bodies escaping the school-to-prison pipeline and are perpetually forced to ask ourselves, *why me?* We cannot speak for the experiences of all students of color or for the varied and diverse experiences of Chicana/o students in predominantly White institutions, but we can present the survival strategies that have contributed to our continued survival. *Entonces amigas/os lo que sigue son consejos que have helped us negotiate varied manifestations of guilt in these academic spaces:*

Primer Consejo: Find a *homeplace* (hooks, 1990). Graduate school is very alienating and it is difficult to be completely separated from your community. *Tu gente te puede ayudar.* Latinas/os are hard to find in these spaces but we are there. If there are no Latina/o graduate organizations, create them! If there are no Latina/o-identified faculty members or students in your program, venture to other disciplines at your university. Reach out to trusted faculty members and their networks. It has often been the case that faculty members connect us nationally with other Latina/o students and faculty members. We make no claims that all Latina/o people in these spaces will turn into a *homeplace*, however, venturing out of our program has enabled us to create spaces of solidarity and allyship that have become sources of strength and empowerment. Our advice to you is to find the space that is going to give you strength in those moments where the feelings of guilt become overwhelming. Connect yourself to bodies and voices that share your experiences, find a space where you don't have to *explain*. Chicana/o authors such as Gloria Anzaldúa, Cherríe Moraga, Michele Serros, Fernando Delgado, and Bernadette Calafell have also provided literary spaces of support and solidarity, for their voices reassure us that we are indeed not alone. *Ya hemos estado aquí, escucha el sonido y las huellas de la gente que marco este lugar como lo nuestro.*

Segundo Consejo: Reach out to the community. Find spaces beyond the walls of the ivory tower that you may be of service to and that can mutually sustain you. The brown bodies in the academy are consumed by the rigor of their program and the alienation that comes with being an underrepresented population in these spaces. Seek people and communities that will provide much needed perspective; *there is life outside of these white walls.* While it may sound like we're advising you to take on more work, believe us when we say that finding non-profit organizations outside of our program has recharged our spirits in profound ways. Having the opportunity to interact with and serve our communities has provided us an outlet to alleviate these overwhelming feelings of guilt. Don't let the ivory tower take your espíritu. *Reach out to your community.* If your intentions are in the right place, they will have a seat for you at the table.

Tercer Consejo: Cuídense así mismo, also known as self-care. Academia can be a hostile and alienating space, so take care of yourself and prioritize your well-being. You do not need to subscribe to the trope of the miserable and damaged graduate student; it will happen on its own if you're not careful. Figure out your non-negotiables and stick to them. If reserving nights for yourself to lounge or to spend time with your partner is important to you, prioritize this time in the construction of your schedule. If eating well is a priority, schedule and commit to spending time each week preparing your meals. If having a social life is important to you, set goals and reward yourself frequently with outings and social gatherings. Play video games, read a non-academic novel, exercise, watch movies; it's okay to take care of yourself. As Chicanas/os we're in spaces that promote feelings of inadequacy and inferiority; the inclination is often to work harder than your peers, to take fewer breaks, and to take on more commitments. This can make taking care of yourself and saying *no* guilt-ridden. Being a Chicana/o graduate student does not mean that you have to place your life on hold. *Live!* Know that this journey is difficult and plagued with work, stress, and feelings of inadequacy. Nada en este mundo es gratis. So take care of yourself and live a lot longer with the people you love most, doing the work you find rewarding.

In writing these final words, we find ourselves in yet another coffee shop. Raisa is editing a paper, and apart from writing these words, I am staring at the stack of finals I have to grade. Raisa's partner is finishing work on his laptop and a friend of ours is busy working on logistics for a conference for a Latina/o graduate organization. We are privileged in that we found a community of Latina/o graduate students. We are privileged in having a group where we can laugh, cry, find solace and mutual support. We hope that you all find this wherever you may/will be going. The struggle is real but the fight is worthwhile. Our bodies need to be in these spaces. Our presence is a political act. Con animo les decimos, hermanas y hermanos si se puede. Se ha dicho y se lograra.

REFERENCES

Amaya, H. (2007). Performing acculturation: Rewriting the Latina/o immigrant self. *Text and Performance Quarterly, 27*(3), 194–212.

Anzaldúa, G. (1999). *Borderlands/La frontera*. San Francisco, CA: Aunt Lute Books.

Calafell, B. M., & Moreman, S. T. (2009). Envisioning an academic readership: Latina/o performativities per the form of publication. *Text and Performance Quarterly, 29*(2), 123–130.

Calafell, B. M., & Moreman, S. T. (2010). Iterative hesitancies and Latinidad: The reverberances of raciality. In T. K. Nakayama & R. T. Halualani (Eds.), *The handbook of critical intercultural communication* (pp. 400–416). Chichester, England; Malden, MA: Wiley-Blackwell.

Delgado, F. (2009). Reflections on being/performing Latino identity in the academy. *Text and Performance Quarterly, 29*(2), 149–164.

Fry, R. (2002). *Latinos in higher education: Many enrol, too few graduate.* Retrieved from Pew Research Center Hispanic Trends website: http://www.pewhispanic.org/files/reports/11.pdf

Griffin, R. A. (2012). I AM an angry Black woman: Black feminist autoethnography, voice, and resistance. *Women's Studies in Communication, 35*(2), 138–157.

hooks, b. (1990). *Yearning: Race, gender and cultural politics.* Boston, MA: South End Press.

Mora, P. (1984). *Chants.* Houston, TX: Arte Publico.

Nora, A., & Crisp, G. (2009). Hispanics and higher education: An overview of research, theory, and practice. In M. B. Paulsen (Ed.), *Higher education: Handbook of theory and research* (pp. 317–353). Rotterdam, The Netherlands: Springer.

Solórzano, D. G., & Yosso, T. J. (2010). Critical race and LatCrit theory and method: Counter-storytelling. *Qualitative Inquiry, 8*(1), 23–44.

Urrieta, L. (2005). "Playing the game" versus "selling out": Chicanas and Chicanos relationship to whitestream schools. In B. K. Alexander, G. L. Anderson, & B. Gallegos (Eds.), *Performance theories in education: Power, pedagogy, and the politics of identity* (pp. 173–196). Mahwah, NJ: Erlbaum.

Urrieta, L., Jr., & Chávez, R. C. (2009). Latin@ faculty in *Academelandia*. In E. G. Murillo Jr. (Ed.), *Handbook of Latinos and education: Theory, research, and practice* (pp. 219–231). New York, NY: Routledge.

Yosso, T. J., & Solórzano, D. G. (2006, March). Leaks in the Chicana & Chicano educational pipeline. *Latino Policy & Issues Brief, 13.* Retrieved from http://www.chicano.ucla.edu/publications/report-brief/leaks-chicana-and-chicano-educational-pipeline

CHAPTER TEN

Navigating Academia's Invisible Margins

Different (dis)Abilities in Graduate Studies

TIMOTHY WELDON

INTRODUCTION

Throughout my academic career, my "different" abilities (or disabilities) have proven to be both my greatest strength and most profound barrier. For much of my life, I was branded "learning disabled," however, with a later diagnosis I learned that I am actually dyslexic—meaning that I process information differently than most people. Dyslexia is often misunderstood as mixing up words and letters, but it is much more dynamic than that. Technically, the diagnosis means certain subsets of a person's cognitive test scores (usually IQ) greatly deviate from the overall level of that person's general score. This type of testing shows cognitive variance that points to different brain functioning and an atypical processing of information. This variance is different for every person. For me, I deviate in reading comprehension and spelling, meaning that I use different parts of my brain than most people to fulfill similar tasks. My diagnosis is significant when trying to "fit" within the specified requirements of academia, as I synthesize, retain, and manage information differently than others and need extra time to produce work at a level commensurate with my overall intellectual abilities.

This is not new. I have struggled with reading my whole life. One of my earliest and most salient memories was finally being allowed to join a reading group with other kids when I was in the second grade. Prior to that there were five reading groups in my class: four groups of varying reading levels, and then "Timmy."

This experience of difference, finally being allowed to join a group, and being segregated because of my disability affected me deeply.

In many careers these differences might not cause issues. However, I have chosen to be a social scientist and my life revolves around reading quickly and strategically to produce high-level intellectual material based on those readings. This situation becomes complicated as no one can *see* dyslexia or my different abilities. Yet within the academic environment and despite processing information differently, I am supposed to understand and retain things as others do.

My academic life has therefore always been a struggle. My grades were never the best, yet I gradually figuring out how to navigate my different abilities and made it through high school. Still, I struggled in college and was finally tested and diagnosed with a learning disability during my second year. My life changed immediately. I have since received a master's degree (and almost a second), had my diagnosis reclassified as dyslexia, and continue to work toward a PhD in anthropology. Yet, I still struggle every day with my different abilities and how they are (or aren't) received by society.

In this chapter I highlight and discuss key issues for graduate students with different abilities to consider within their studies. First, it is important to be *tested* for "different abilities," and seek out professional advice (and encouragement) based on your diagnosis. As a differently abled student it is paramount that you learn your strengths and find comfort with this aspect of who you are. Keep in mind that you are being asked to fit your brain and body into a world governed by what works for "normal" people. Just because you don't fit the ideal of what people in the academy expect doesn't mean you don't have a tremendous amount to offer. A key aspect of navigating academia will be making people see you and your abilities as a strength, not a weakness (or a hassle).

The second major hurdle you will face is whether to *disclose* your different abilities (both within the application process and/or once you've enrolled). There are numerous prejudices that people with different (dis)abilities face, so you have to be careful and strategic. Always remember that in some way you will consistently be working "against the system," and must learn to engage strategically within its institutionalized norms. The third key is receiving *accommodation* for your different (dis)abilities. Getting help can make an immense difference in graduate school. For example, I recently started using software that cut my reading time by a third.

The fourth and fifth issues surround other peoples' *ideologies* and *accommodation*, and educational cultures and learning environments that are inherently designed by and for a "majority" that are without disabilities. Within these environments of accommodation it is easy for administrators and faculty members to assume the issue is solved and they do not need to treat you differently. In short, accommodation can provide the illusion of equality, while simultaneously not *solving* the larger entrenched societal issues you will face at school. This tends to close space for different learning styles and act instead to assimilate (and neutralize) people with different abilities into thinking and being more like the majority. This is an issue exacerbated by the hierarchical nature of student-teacher relationships that leads to a lack of awareness and little impetus among faculty and administrators to understand people with "special" needs.

TESTING

Not having been tested and diagnosed when I was a child, my formative educational years were a struggle. When I was finally tested in college I was said to be "learning disabled," which offered a clearly defined issue to develop learning strategies around. I did not yet understand the nuances of what being "disabled" meant, but I received accommodation for extra time on tests and assignments; new techniques for learning; and a restructured course load more commensurate with my learning style. My grades went up immediately and I started making the honor roll. Getting tested changed my intellectual trajectory, even if I didn't yet understand my disability and its strengths.

It wasn't until I tried to go back to graduate school 10 years later that I underwent further testing, and received a whole new perspective on my "disability." Rather than the test administrator telling me what I should not do, I was told what I *could* do. I learned that I "process information differently," *not wrongly*. I was dyslexic, *not* stupid—just different. I felt like I was in a comic book, where a kid ostracized their whole life for being different is finally told by someone that not only are they not a freak because of their unique abilities, but they actually have exceptional powers! (Yes, I learned to read with superhero comic books!)

When the man who administered the test discussed my results, he told me about Leonardo da Vinci, Albert Einstein, and other successful people who were dyslexic. He explained to me that I had managed academically because I was in fact incredibly smart and created different connections and ways of learning with the rest of my intellect to compensate for the different way my brain functioned. I walked out of his office finally feeling like I belonged, like my intellect had something to offer (rather than being something to hide), and I had a reason to be confident in myself academically. After being tested, I began testing boundaries, feeling comfortable challenging existing paradigms.

DISCLOSURE

This feeling of empowerment unfortunately did not immediately extend to how others viewed me and people with different (dis)abilities in general. Society has its prejudices, and when I first applied to graduate school (before my dyslexia diagnosis) I saw myself as disabled, and grappled with how and when to tell people and schools this. Disclosing different abilities—or *disabilities*—both within the application process and following admission is very tricky to navigate. How do you know you won't be profiled and dismissed outright over societal misperceptions?

In the first graduate program I attended I did not tell anyone that I was learning disabled nor ask for accommodation at any point (despite specifically going to school in England because standardized testing was not required). However, without extra time and support I struggled to keep up, I couldn't get my papers in on time, and I handed in my thesis a semester late.

Still, I received my MA and (with a hint of confidence) looked to continue toward a PhD. I started opening up about what I still saw as my learning disability, only to be *shockingly* put in my place. While in the United States I met with a professor I was interested in working with. We had a great conversation, and he sent me to the departmental administrator for information about applying for the "University Professor's Program" (an elite multidisciplinary program at that university). Everything was going well until I asked the administrator whether the Graduate Record Examinations (GREs) were mandatory. She replied, "Yes, of course they are." I responded disappointedly, but in my usual playfully open (and naively confident) manner, that standardized tests were tough for me because I was learning disabled. She was taken aback, and looked at me incredulously, saying: "Oh, well, there's no place in the University Professor's Program for people with learning disabilities." I don't even remember my response or the rest of the conversation. I just remember feeling so wonderful about the meeting with the professor, then being told by this administrator that I could never be good enough for that program. I walked away, and never followed up with the professor. I felt crushed.

But in retrospect, was the problem what she said, or that I didn't have the confidence (or the understanding of my diagnosis) to feel empowered enough to stand up and present a more comprehensive view of the nuances and *gifts* of how my dyslexic brain worked? After the first diagnosis I saw myself as "disabled" and didn't have much intellectual confidence. With the second diagnosis, I immediately became "dyslexic," and began to see my differences as an asset. I was the same person, my brain functioned the same way, but I saw myself differently and approached school and people differently. Had I known my strengths better and felt more confident in them, I could have spoken to that administrator of my diagnosis, disclosing my strengths in a way that sold my differences as a positive rather than something to cower behind.

I honed my application strategy for PhD programs over the next 5 years, putting in three rounds of applications before finally being accepted. During that interim period I had the second test. Although I still did not disclose my diagnosis in those initial applications, I took a different approach several years later, applying locally with a focus on developing relationships with faculty in my area and selectively and carefully disclosing my dyslexia. I got closer, but was rejected again. Following this, I changed my entire approach. I concentrated on developing personal relationships and visiting with faculty at schools with similar interests to mine. Also, I not only disclosed my dyslexia, but I also owned it, marketed it, and explained it at length as a strength that I could uniquely offer. If I was going to fail to get into a PhD program one last time, it was going to be the *real me* that didn't get in. I received offers from three schools—the three I visited most and where I developed the best relationships.

Without meeting or getting to know someone at a given school, all the admissions committee knew about me was what was on paper: suspect grades, average test scores, and a host of interesting life experience. I learned I will not win the academic application process on paper. Rather, I have to show people exactly what my strengths are: my grades are low because I am dyslexic, and I do things differently and analyze things differently because my brain processes things differently. I have charisma, I have passion, I have the interpersonal skills needed to be a great anthropologist, and I work harder than most people because *there is no other way for me to succeed.* I needed prospective professors to *see* these strengths.

If you have different abilities, show how you and your abilities can contribute to a given program, making their department stronger. Find a way to disclose, express, promote, and use your different abilities as strengths. If you do not disclose, the application committee will measure you against everyone else—without knowing that your grades may not convey the unique assets and strengths you bring as a student. Remember, the application process is subjective, and evaluations often depend on the individual reading your application. By not disclosing, you are saying you are the same as everyone else. Which may, in turn, actually "handicap" your possibilities for no reason other than the fear that you will be discriminated against. Which may happen, but all it takes is one person who sees the merits of your differences. I now actively disclose and fight for my rights at all costs. I know I am different—and *you want my kind of difference* at your school!

ACCOMMODATION

This is not to say that this difference comes without its issues. I still have to get work done within a system not designed for me. Yet with a few simple accommodations people with different (dis)abilities can work more easily within their system. I understand that it may be difficult to be seen as different or to ask for help. However, the world, academia, and your career don't care about your pride, only your results. The intellectual world is asking you to *not* do things naturally.

Laws about accommodation are there for a reason; they are designed to facilitate you functioning as something you are not—but need to become if you want to be successful in this career. There is no shame in seeking out support and making use of every program that can help you, even if only as a tool to try to eventually change the system.

For me, accommodation entails extra time on tests and assignments, and the use of alternative text formats that read documents aloud as I read a hard copy. Not only do I retain information better, but I read a third faster. There are some complications though. I need reading lists months in advance (which can annoy faculty) and it takes time to get or scan electronic copies of readings. The extra time is helpful but also has drawbacks. If I take extra time one week, I fall behind with the next week's assignments. As a result, I rarely ask for extra time (mostly using it for final papers or a couple of hours), and instead hand in rushed work I consider below the standards I am accustomed to.

There are also other drawbacks to this, though, as accommodation does not change the structural and cultural issues ingrained within society that turn "difference" into "disability," and opportunity into prejudice. With accommodation, people with "disabilities" are afforded compensatory opportunities to level the playing field in relation to other "able"-bodied or -minded people. Yet, just as affirmative action has not "fixed" racism, accommodation does not "fix" the social and educational challenges people with different abilities face. These diagnoses are social constructs inextricably linked to learning and academic environments; for it is within the classroom that students and children become differentiated based on both their successes and struggles.

PEDAGOGY AND LEARNING STYLES

Throughout my entire life these dominant structures of learning have proven to be one of my main challenges. Every aspect of the way we learn—from reading-centric curriculums, standardized testing, and hyper-competitive grading systems to hierarchical classrooms, vertical pedagogies, and the way we structure our courses and course loads—is a socially constructed product of pedagogies and learning styles inherently produced by and for those in positions of power. I mean, what if our learning environment was communal; openly crowd-sourcing knowledge in ways less concerned about authors and individual arguments and more focused on building broader, more inclusive and non-commoditized forms of knowledge? Our systems of learning and teaching have evolved and been largely produced within the character of the majority of people, and therefore circuitously benefit those who can more easily work within those dominant learning styles. Based on their minority status (and therefore simple probability), people who learn differently are at a disadvantage and less likely to succeed and/or rise to influential positions that can then effect future teaching methods. As a result, those in positions of power tend to be of the more typically abled majority and more likely to be comfortable with "the way things are." As the concept of different abilities is largely overlooked in mainstream Western social narratives, there is also little impetus for people who have been successful in the current system to think about including or accounting for people with different abilities. If they were, the academy (and Western learning styles) would look very different, already having made it easier for people with different abilities to excel. As disability scholar Simi Linton says, both as a society and academy we have allowed "disabled" people to be "hidden."

Whether in the institutions that have confined us, the attics and basements that sheltered our family's shame, the "special" schools and classrooms designed to solve the problems we are thought to represent, or riding in segregated transportation, those "invalid" coaches that shuttle disabled people from one of these venues to another, we are hidden. The public has become so used to these screens that as we are now emerging, upping the ante on the demands for a truly inclusive society, we disrupt the social order. We further confound expectations when we have the temerity to emerge as forthright and resourceful people, nothing like the self-loathing, docile, bitter, or insentient fictional versions of ourselves the public is more used to (Linton, 1998).

And just as we are hidden from everyday life, our learning needs are largely hidden from mainstream teaching pedagogies. The very basis of academic curricula, with their focus on publishing written books and articles, is not designed to include people who struggle with written materials. It then becomes up to those who process information differently to conform to a world whose mechanisms we are only just starting to shape. As a graduate school student you must recognize that the entire learning environment is designed for someone who probably does not think like you, and in all likelihood does not even realize (or comprehend) that you think differently. Most faculty members and students are unlikely to have had much professional contact with people with different abilities and will likely not "see" people with disabilities, especially invisible ones. As such, you may struggle getting others to accept the validity and merits of the different perspectives and understandings you bring to the classroom.

Those who you interact with daily will also likely be unaware of the structural violence and prejudices found within their own pedagogies or the social dynamics that surround different (dis)abilities. No amount of accommodation will keep someone from saying or thinking that "there is no place for you" here, or being unwittingly hurtful about why you don't ever have time to read other' work or go out, or where you get certain ideas or how you may take class discussions in different directions than professors and students see as relevant. Of course I take things in different directions! I process information and comprehend readings differently than others because my brain works differently than theirs! So, inherently, I offer different insights that may seem tangential or harder for others to relate to. These misunderstandings do not make your colleagues bad people, just part of a normally abled society that generally lacks knowledge of how to engage with people with different (dis)abilities.

ACADEMIC POWER DYNAMICS

This lack of awareness about invisible disabilities is exacerbated when coupled with the hierarchy and egotism that is pervasive in academia, especially the hierarchical nature of student-teacher relationships. Many faculty members—particularly at research universities—teach because it is a condition of their research positions, and therefore necessary for their livelihoods. For many, the teaching aspect of their professorship is a *job*, not a passion. It's important to recognize that this job comes with a lot of pressures: conducting research, publishing original work, teaching students, grading papers, running departments, and reviewing peers' work. And while you will gain insight and knowledge from faculty members, you should not be surprised if they behave like their time is more valuable than yours (partly because, in monetary terms, it is). Ultimately, faculty members do not have a lot of extra time, and you are not their first (or last) graduate student. This is especially true for students who have "special" needs and ask for adjustments and alterations that require additional effort and time of professors. While some may welcome the challenge, you need to be prepared for push back from them.

Your professors simply may not be accustomed to being asked for "special treatment" by students, nor respect this as the best use of their time, especially given the complicated structural considerations inherent within the student-teacher relationship. Academic success requires years of tireless work accumulating a very specialized type of highly valued and commoditized knowledge. Armed with this privileged position of knowledge, professors are then paid to stand in front of young adults attentively staring up at them with curious and rapt eyes, hanging on every word—as if their future depends on it! And it does! The teacher has ultimate power and decides how well students have "learned" the "right" knowledge.

This authority is reinforced by the tenure system, in which professors at major research universities are largely unhindered by how well they teach and the manner in which they engage with students. While tenure is an important system designed to provide freedom from persecution and encourage intellectual freedom, this structure also leads to relatively little accountability or space for students to voice concerns. For example, in my current department there is no institutionalized means for graduate student feedback on either advisors or the program. This is compounded by the almost guild-like structure found within the academic training process, within which you (the apprentice) must learn how to become a professor by emulating your guild-master and making him or her like (or respect) you enough to help get you job opportunities throughout your entire professional career. But the fundamental paradox students with different abilities face is how does a person with different abilities emulate someone so intellectually dissimilar from them, all the while using a style not innate to them? If you learn differently, produce knowledge differently, and think differently than someone, how in turn can you ever really emulate them? Yet you are still expected to. And should you struggle with this or them at any point, and stand up against these established power structures, you should be prepared for backlash, disappointment, and even possible isolation.

CONCLUSION

As a graduate student with invisible (dis)abilities you will be challenged both personally and institutionally. You will struggle to find knowledgeable allies and sympathetic faculty. You are going to be different and people may struggle to notice (or even care) to understand why. But if people with different (dis)abilities are to have more allies and academia is to have more inclusive pedagogies, we must rise above these challenges. We have to get tested; learn, embrace, and promote our strengths; take comfort in who we are; use the accommodation given to us; be open about our skills, needs, and how we are affected by society's prejudices; and claim space for our different (dis)abilities. Only through this embracing of our vibrant and diverse selves can we create niches for more people with different (dis)abilities to complete their studies; therefore disrupting the social order in a way that creates a new academy—inclusive of a safe space for people with any multitude of (dis)abilities.

REFERENCES

Ginsburg F., & Rapp, R. (2013). Disability worlds. *Annual Review of Anthropology, 42*, 53–68.

Ingstad, B., & Reynolds, W. S. (1995). *Disability and culture.* Berkeley, CA: University of California Press.

Kasnitz, D., Switzer, M., & Shuttleworth, R. P. (2001). Introduction: Anthropology in disability studies. *Disability Studies Quarterly, 21*(3).

Linton, S. (1998). *Claiming disability: Knowledge and identity.* New York, NY: New York University Press.

Raphael, D., Salovesh, M., & Laclave, M. (2001). The world in 3D: Dyslexia, dysgraphia, dysnumia. *Disability Studies Quarterly, 21*(3).

Ruby Reid-Cunningham, A. (2009). Anthropological theories of disability. *Journal of Human Behavior in the Social Environment, 19*, 99–111.

CHAPTER ELEVEN

A Working-Class Chicana Navigating a PhD Program While Feeling Like an Impostor

YESSICA GARCIA HERNANDEZ

INTRODUCTION: FEELING LIKE AN IMPOSTOR

Have you ever felt like an impostor in your own university? Maybe because of the way you speak, the way you look, or the location of your school?

The impostor phenomenon has been described as an internal experience of intellectual fakeness that is prevalent among high achieving women (Clance & Imes, 1978). It is common for people who experience the impostor syndrome to believe that they are not really that intelligent and that they have been mistakenly admitted to graduate school (Clance & Imes, 1978). As a working-class Latina, I have felt like an impostor in the universities I have attended because of my racial, cultural, and class identities. Feeling like an impostor in graduate school is a daily feeling for me. At first I thought I was the only person feeling these emotions. Although I read everything assigned for class, I walked into seminars feeling terrified about not reading enough material for the discussion that day. I constantly asked myself whether I was the only person who struggled reading authors such as Gayatri Spivak, or if I was the only one looking up definitions of words and key terms I did not understand from the text. These thoughts tormented me until I confessed these feelings to my advisors and both of them told me that the impostor syndrome is very common in academia (particularly among students of color) and it might never go away. My reply to my advisors was, "Really?!" One told me, "you will always feel it, it does not stop after you graduate you will feel it in your first job, while you go up for tenure, after you get tenure, when asking for a promotion, all the time." So if it never goes away, what must we do to minimize the impostor voice in our head and not let it immobilize us?

Using a *testimonio* approach, I share what programs enabled me to prepare for graduate school, the activities I engaged in to navigate the impostor syndrome, and some of the advice that mentors and advisors have shared with me to survive graduate school. I emphasize the impostor syndrome because that is something that I struggle with constantly. I share my story in order to give a snapshot of the emotional ride you may experience in graduate school. These techniques have helped me navigate graduate school as a working-class Chicana doctoral student.

ABOUT ME: A WORKING-CLASS CHICANA

I am the first person in my Mexican immigrant family to graduate from college. To help my father during my mother's deportation to Mexico, I started working when I was 13 years old, and my high school grade point average was barely a 1.0 (out of a 4.00 scale). I never imagined obtaining a university degree, let alone doing research and enrolling in a doctoral program. After high school, I enrolled in a local community college, and my grades improved. I joined a transfer program to get advice and mentorship about navigating the community college system, since over 30% of students take more than 6 years to transfer (Ruiz, 2015). At the community college level, I was very confident about my academic abilities. I was proud about staying in college since many of my friends had dropped out because they did not qualify for financial aid. In 2 years, I managed to complete all my remedial college classes, and successfully passed all my transfer classes with a 3.5 grade point average. I was very proud of myself. During my community college days, I did not suffer from the impostor syndrome. Feeling like an impostor started when I transferred to a tier-1 research university.

I was not warned that I was going to embark on such an emotional rollercoaster; for a couple of quarters I made the mistake of allowing the impostor syndrome to paralyze me, and I felt very intimidated by the process of research and writing. In those days, I did not have a thick skin for the micro-aggressions I heard in the classrooms. In fact, I didn't even know what the term micro-aggression was. The higher I went in the educational pipeline, the more of a stranger I felt because there were only a few working-class Latinas there too. Studies have documented that less than 1% of Latinas obtain a doctoral degree (Castellanos, Alberta, & Kamimura, 2006, p. 114). The low number of Latinas and, more broadly, women of color in academia is one of the reasons why I feel that I am an impostor and that I might not belong there. What has helped me navigate the impostor syndrome is recognizing the first time I felt like an impostor. For me, the feelings started as an undergraduate when I transferred to the University of California, because I met students from different ethnicities and social classes. Unlike me, many of them knew early on that they were going to go to a university and had high expectations from the university. Although I was not in graduate school yet, a mild form of the impostor syndrome started with that feeling of indebtedness to the university. I felt that I did not fully believe in my potential. Even if professors told me that my papers were great, I would not believe them. I was my own worst enemy. I doubted in my abilities and felt that I had to work harder to prove to everyone that I deserved to be there. Once you start thinking like an impostor it is really hard to stop; I've graduated twice (BA and MA) and I still think I am an impostor sometimes. In retrospect, there were some helpful things that I did as an undergraduate student that helped me feel less like an impostor in my master's program, such as participating in a summer research program and creating an honor thesis.

THE PIPELINE: PREDOCTORAL PROGRAMS

In my second year at the university I met a literature professor who uses Chicana feminism and theater to talk about violence and trauma within the Latino community. I immediately felt inspired by her pedagogy. Because of my hard work in class, the professor invited me to apply to a Mentoring Summer Research Internship Program (MSRIP) that would demystify research, the graduate record exam (GRE), and how to apply to graduate school. I applied, and was one of 20 students selected to participate in the 8-week research program. When the program started and I met other students from different universities, and most of them knew exactly what their career path was going to be. Their levels of confidence made me insecure, and the first thing that came to my mind was again rooted in that impostor syndrome. "Why did I get chosen?," I asked myself. "Did they confuse my application with someone else's?" As I am writing this, those words sound silly to me, and I feel embarrassed for admitting that these thoughts existed in my mind especially when my advice is that summer research programs help you understand graduate school. Now I know from talking to others that these thoughts are more common than we think they are. I felt I did not belong in that program because I did not have everything figured out like the other students, or so it seemed. If you ever participate in a pipeline program and notice that other students seem more prepared for graduate school, do not feel bad like I did.

I regret not voicing my feelings to my advisor and program coordinator at the time because I did not want to be judged or associated with weakness and failure. The last thing I wanted was for people to think that I was going to drop out of something before I had even started. The ironic part of this is that due to all the earlier experiences with the impostor syndrome, I have now reached a level of confidence regarding the graduate school process, and I now *know* that I belong in academia. I have no doubt about that. I now recognize that they did not mistakenly accept me; they chose me because I have a lot of new insights that I can contribute to my field of discipline. What enabled me to get to that point of security was reflecting a lot about my feelings, listening very carefully to what other students had experienced, and asking a lot of questions about graduate school. Every time I felt insecure, I had to pause and tell myself, "Yessica, remember that we all have different stories—we all apply to graduate school for different reasons!" Telling myself this every time I felt insecure helped me remember that I was not doing things wrong, or late. If you also find yourself feeling frustrated, tell yourself similar comments: "I am not an impostor and I applied, or want to apply, to graduate school because I have something to say!"

VENTING GROUPS AND SAFE CIRCLES

Sometimes, talking about the impostor syndrome will be hard because you may not have a sincere conversation about it with everyone. It is very common that some students will perform a level of confidence and pretend everything is well. However, graduate school may have a tendency to make you lose confidence in yourself because you will be relearning how to view knowledge, and your department will be training you to become a producer of knowledge. Feelings of insecurity will be normal, and the first step to control these feelings is to talk about them in a safe circle where you will not be judged.

Resource centers and psychological services offered by your institution are an excellent way to find a community of students who are willing to be honest about their insecurities. Finding a place where you can go after class or when you are feeling down is very important. For me, my safe space is the Raza Resource Center (RRC) on campus. The RRC is a center that focuses on supporting Chicana/o and Latina/o students on campus. After a bad day, I go there and talk to the director of the program. The director of the center is one of my mentors on campus. Because he is a person of color, I know I can talk to him about my insecurities and moments of doubts, since he is not going to judge me. Find mentors and advisors who are also outside of your department. This is very important because sometimes you need to talk to people who can see things differently and who can give you advice from a neutral position. Although it is very important to build relationships within your department, it is a good idea to have a venting circle outside your department too.

I have mentors from the School of Medicine, music, communication, sociology, and women's studies. Sometimes you meet these mentors at events where you least expect it. During my first quarter in the doctoral program, I attended a workshop about funding, specifically about applying to the Ford Foundation. In this workshop I met a professor from the School of Medicine, who I never thought would advise me. After the workshop I asked him if I could e-mail him to schedule an appointment to meet and talk more about writing fellowships. He agreed and we met soon after the workshop. During our meeting, he helped me rewrite my application and gave me a lot of feedback about the structure and organization of writing grants. As I was preparing to leave he told me, "See. You probably never imagined that a professor from the School of Medicine could help you." The professor was right. I would have never imagined receiving so much advice from a professor outside of my discipline. Networking and reaching out for help is crucial in graduate school. If a professor offers to help you or tells you "e-mail me," make sure that you do just that—e-mail the professor and follow up on the conversation.

If a safe circle or resource center does not exist in your school, you can create your own. Two ideas might be to create a student organization on campus or to ask the psychological services on campus to help you create a venting/therapy group. When I was doing my MA in Chicana/o Studies at California State University, I was part of an organization called MALCS: *Mujeres Activas en Letras y Cambio Social.* That student group was my safe circle. I knew that every time I met with the other group members, I was able to say what I felt about the graduate process without being judged. Currently, there is no MALCS at the university that I attend, but my goal is to create that space again so I can continue to have a safe space for women of color.

The psychological services on campus are another great resource because therapy can help you a lot during graduate school. If you are someone who doesn't trust people easily, especially when talking about personal vulnerabilities, going to therapy might be a good idea for you because everything is confidential. It is important that you have someone to share those feelings with, and a therapist is a good place to start. A friend told me once that choosing a therapist who has experience with graduate students is a good idea because they will know how to help you more.

Another place where you can find a community is at national conferences. During a recent conference I participated in a roundtable at the National Women Studies Association, where some of my colleagues and I spoke about the Latina/o educational pipeline. The roundtable was very intimate, which gave us an opportunity to create mentorship relationships and talk about the marginalities we were experiencing at our universities. Some of the participants shared that being part of a women-of-color group on campus helped them overcome the pain of encountering micro-aggressions and the impostor syndrome that they felt. In their study, Allen and Solórzano (2001) found that racial stereotypes remind students of color of their "otherness" in the university. Micro-aggressions is the term often used to describe these subtle expressions of racism and sexism. These comments often repeat or affirm demeaning stereotypes about a minority group (Davila, 2015).

In my case, because I am doing a doctoral program in Ethnic Studies, my seminar experience in my department is a safe space in comparison to other departments where they only have one "diverse" student. All of the professors in my department are conscious about race, racism, and liberal multiculturalism. Thus, for the most part, I always feel safe to express my thoughts. It is usually when I take classes in other disciplines and during graduate student association events that I feel marginalized and belittled for being a working-class Chicana in academia. In other departments and classrooms I am usually the only woman of color in the room. Sometimes I try to forget my difference with the hopes of not feeling so self-conscious, but just when I am about to do that, my own professors and/or classmates remind me of my "uniqueness." Their comments always make me nervous and self-conscious about what I should say and do. After these classes finish, I always go back to the Raza Resource Center to re-energize and remind myself why I am in graduate school. I try not to internalize negative comments that I receive. Inside the RRC, I feel safe about talking about graduate school.

Two concerns of mine that I share with people at the RRC are the homeland security checkpoint near my university and my anxiety about writing. Due to what, in reality, is a militarized checkpoint, many of my close friends cannot come visit me on campus. Because of nationality and anti-immigrant sentiments, the possibility of family deportations is a common struggle among Latina/o students in my university. Prior to accepting admission at my university, I did not think much about the consequences the militarized checkpoint would have for me afterwards. As it is, graduate school already helps you create social barriers among you and your family because you have an excessive workload. Adding a physical border is that much harder. If you are an undocumented student, or have undocumented family members who are important to you and want them around for your college years, please take the location of your university into consideration when accepting an offer. Call the student services at the campus where you are planning to attend and ask them about the services that they offer for undocumented students and family members. Also, visit the resource centers on campus to talk to other students in similar situations and ask them how they are coping with these issues. My university, for example, has a website that focuses on serving undocumented students. The university that you are interested in attending might have a website too.

This year I helped create and organize the Raza Writing Collective (RWC) at the RRC. The RWC meets every Friday at noon, and its mission is to collectively minimize writing anxieties. The meetings take place at the conference room where we check in with each other each week about how we are feeling and how we are progressing. During our first meeting, we read the first chapter of a book titled *Writing Your Journal Article in Twelve Weeks* by Wendy Laura Belcher (2009). If you have anxieties about writing, I strongly recommend this book because it gives you a guideline to follow about the process of writing an academic text. The philosophy behind this book is that you have to follow the rule of writing consistently; for example, writing just 15 minutes a day will take you a long way. We followed the book's instructions and committed ourselves to writing consistently and it worked! Many of us felt more comfortable about our writing after just 10 weeks. Most of the students in our collective agreed that the voice of the impostor pops up the most when you're in front of the computer writing. In the writing collective, we help each other cope with those feelings and we advise each other on what we can do to avoid letting those feelings paralyze us. I am really glad that I have the RWC as a space where I can share these emotions and not be judged. In my graduate student career, I have learned that insecurity is a common feeling for me. Sometimes my insecurity might be due to my writing and other times the insecurity comes from not knowing if I am going to see a friend again because of the militarized checkpoint. Regardless of the reason, I continue to fight every day to feel confident about my voice and my contributions to the academy. The secret for achieving that confidence is self-care, particularly if, like me, you also feel like an impostor. A study found that the clinical symptoms associated with the impostor syndrome include, "generalized anxiety, lack of self-confidence, depression, and frustration related to the inability to meet self-imposed standards of achievement" (Clance & Imes, 1978, p. 242). Let's try not to fall into these clinical symptoms.

CONCLUSION: ENGAGING IN SELF-CARE

While reading this chapter you cannot hear or see the many times I've visited and talked to my therapist, mentor, and closest colleagues about my struggles with believing that I belong in graduate school. There were many times where I visited them to even talk about my ability to write this chapter. However, after I heard my advisor tell me that the impostor syndrome will never go away, I found ways to overcome those feelings. I hope that my experiences help you navigate graduate school in a healthy way and help you avoid making some of the mistakes that I made in regards to not trusting and believing in my abilities. Nonetheless, if you only remember one thing from this chapter, remember that self-care is the number one rule to survive graduate school. To reiterate that rule, I cite Audrey Lorde (1988), "[c]aring for myself is not self-indulgence, it is self-preservation, and that is an act of political warfare" (p. 131). If the impostor syndrome will not go away, like my advisor told me, then we must find healthy ways to take care of ourselves and find a community that believes in us, reminds us that our attendance in graduate school is important, and reminds us that we deserve to be there.

Self-care is different for everyone. There are cultural and racial implications of self-care, so sit down for a minute and figure out what self-care means to you. Think about the activities that make you happy. Do you enjoy a day at the spa?

Do you enjoy dancing, zumba, or playing an instrument? Do you enjoy watching webisodes or TV? Do you enjoy playing videogames? Graduate school can easily make you feel that you do not have time to engage in any fun activity. There have been many occasions when I have, for example, gone to the gym and as soon as I get there, I think about the millions of things that I could be doing if I was not there such as reading, taking notes, writing my class responses, looking for conferences to present at, searching for fellowships, and so on. There have been moments where I actually do leave the gym after thinking, "I could be reading right now!" However, the constant feeling of misusing time is not healthy. There will always be an extra book you need to read. There will always be an extra paper or e-mail you have to write. That does not mean that you do not deserve, or should not make time for, self-care.

The times when I left the gym early made my week feel miserable and neverending. I was not happy because I did not give myself a break. Breaks are very important for you. Something that I started doing recently is creating a rewards program for myself. When I work really hard and finish my tasks I treat myself to something that I like, which can be a material object or an activity. I have a deadline list, and along with the deadline I also write down the reward that I will give myself after I accomplish my task. My reward for finishing this book chapter was purchasing a sound adapter for my filmmaking equipment. Try the reward system, I promise that it will work. As you have read in my *testimonio*, I am surviving graduate school because I have a lot of mentors and advisors that talk to me about their own experiences. Graduate school can be a very frustrating place for a woman of color, but it has become a political decision to not let the impostor syndrome paralyze me and defeat me. Never forget that it does not matter how we get to the finish line, as long as we get there.

REFERENCES

Allen, W. R., & Solórzano, D. (2001). Affirmative action, educational equity, and campus racial climate: A case study of the University of Michigan Law School. *Berkeley Raza Law Journal, 12*(2), 237–363.

Belcher, W. L. (2009). *Writing your journal article in twelve weeks: A guide to academic publishing success.* Thousand Oaks, CA: Sage.

Castellanos, J., Alberta, M. G., & Kamimura, M. (Eds.). (2006). *The Latina/o pathways to the Ph.D Abriendo Caminos.* Sterling, VA: Stylus.

Clance, P. R., & Imes, S. A. (1978). The impostor phenomenon in high achieving women: Dynamics and therapeutic interventions. *Psychotherapy: Theory, Research and Practice, 15*(8), 241–247.

Davila, B. (2015). Critical race theory, disability microaggressions and Latina/o student experiences in special education. *Race Ethnicity and Education, 18*(4), 443–468.

Gibson-Beverly, G., & Schwartz, J. (2008). Attachment, entitlement, and the impostor phenomenon in female graduate students. *Journal of College Counseling, 11*(2), 119–132.

Lorde, A. (1988). *A burst of light: Essays.* Ithaca, NY: Firebrand Books.

Muhs, G. G., Flores Niemann, Y., Gonzalez, C., & Harris, A. P. (Eds.). (2012). *Presumed incompetent: The intersections of race and class for women in academia.* Boulder, CO: University Press of Colorado.

Roché, J. (2014). Conquering impostor syndrome: Lessons from female and minority business leaders. *Leader to Leader, 2014*(74), 13–18.

Ruiz, J. (2015, May 27). LBCC figures show "unacceptable" six-year path to transfer. *Long Beach Post.* Retrieved from http://lbpost.com/news/education/2000006196-lbcc-transfer-rates

CHAPTER TWELVE

Dis / Advantage

Finding the Middle
Between High-Achieving and Hell

LARA ROSE ROBERTS

INTRODUCTION: BIPOLAR DICHOTOMIES

I had been doing fine without medication for a quarter of a century, and I wanted to believe the research from the stack of books I had checked out from the library that suggested I might even owe my academic and professional honors to this disordered brain functioning.

I was diagnosed with bipolar II disorder the year before starting graduate school, and looking back at my life, I could see that my periods of peak productivity might have been caused by hypomanic highs, though I had never been concerned, because I enjoyed the overwhelming elation from my grade point average or promotions at work. I could also see that my procrastination might have been amplified by depression: I pushed projects until well beyond the last minute so that I would have an adrenaline fix to pull myself out of apathy and back into my life.

I assumed that graduate school would simply be more of the same undulations, and I assumed I would be able to self-manage. After all, as long as the highs continued to dictate success, then the lows did not matter. I just needed to manage my hypomanic time more effectively.

My fallacy, though, was thinking that there would be weeks in graduate school when I could afford not to be "on." My other fallacy was in thinking of time management in a More effective/Less effective dichotomy, rather than as Possible versus Impossible. In my disordered brain, any semblance of order or time management was unreasonable. The only order with which I structured my life was Success versus Failure, and I know I am not the only high-achiever who holds myself to those standards. The problem is, in that dichotomy, it is impossible to admit to struggling. To ask for help is to admit defeat.

What I could not see was that a healthy, successful life is one in which standard dichotomies can break down—especially the one between success and failure, because that dichotomy also tends to divide the world between Me and Everyone Else. Human civilization is built on the concept of We—We are all in this together, and we should not let ourselves hit the lowest low before we ask for help. This becomes all the more important during graduate school, when mental health problems become exacerbated from the stress of having to do more on less sleep than many other points in our lives. The first year in particular pushes us to the edge of our mental capabilities. The goal of graduate school is success, but to get there, you must know the limits of your mental health and you must ask for help before you reach them.

I didn't, and 25 years of "doing fine" almost fell apart because of it.

In this chapter, I will stress the importance of self-awareness, self-advocacy, *and* awareness and advocacy for others, in terms of mental health. I have used my own experiences from the year I started my graduate program in order to show how important it is to bolster awareness of mental health. The middle section of this chapter is written as creative non-fiction and thus will likely feel more personal than other advice you might have read about how to succeed in graduate school. However, even if your program is not in a humanities department like mine, we must remember how important the human factor is to *all* graduate programs.

HYPOMANIC ADVANTAGE

"During the period of mood disturbance and increased energy and activity, three or more of the following symptoms must have persisted and must have been present to a significant degree.

Increase in goal-directed activity

    either socially

    at work

    or school

    or sexually.

Decreased need for sleep

    feels rested after only 3 hours.

Inflated self-esteem or grandiosity.

More talkative than usual.

Flight of ideas.

Distractibility.

Individuals with bipolar II disorder may not view the hypomanic episodes as pathological or disadvantageous

others may be troubled by the individual's erratic behavior."

(American Psychiatric Association, 2013, pp. 132–135)

January February March

These were the months that I finished applications to graduate school and acceptance letters began arriving. My eyes were wide and all I could see was Success in my future. This positive outlook seems like it would be a normal reaction for anyone. Even psychologists agree that the symptoms of bipolar mania read as characteristics that seem inherent to anyone with a drive for success *or grandiosity*. I considered my drive to be an advantage, though when I talked to my psychiatrist about the diagnosis, I remember thinking it strange that he knew that my productivity and creativity always came in waves of unpredictable, uncontainable *goal-directed activity*.

I did not realize that energy was symptomatic of hypomania
energy like the waves at high tide when it is better to stay off the beach.

But I was the wave.

always more

always better

April May June July

I started a new job, one that I had been positive I would get from the minute I submitted my résumé that listed bullets detailing my *inflated self-esteem*.

My psychiatrist was concerned I was not sleeping.

I was delighted at the projects I could finish.

He continued to suggest medication to me.

I showed him research on the side effects.

He said that the way I functioned in my bipolar waves might not be sustainable.

I said lethargy was not sustainable, and I stopped going to my appointments.

decreased need for sleep

is always better

I was the nighttime

better

August/September

Classes started, and I thought I might be at a disadvantage for taking 4 years off to work professionally after my bachelor's degree. I hardly remembered how to read academic writing and the other students threw theorists' names around like they were Facebook friends. But in class, I was *more talkative than usual*, the first to answer a question or suggest an interpretation, my *flight of ideas* were impressive, and I never showed up to class without having done the reading. If graduate school was a game, I was sure that I was going to win it.

When I complained to my mother about how long the reading assignments took me,

I was *distractible*

I averaged 30 minutes per page

she told me the first semester of graduate school is like a sieve. She said that every discipline has their versions of Research Methods and Introduction to Theory that function to separate the fine scholars who *will* make it from the coarse extras who will not. In my manic fog, the sieve was Failure and the perforations at the end of the semester were shaped like Success; I looked at my peers as though they were coarse grit, and I did not understand why they all seemed so tired.

I was part of the heterogeneous mixture,

and more energy

and less sleep

made me fine

a fine scholar

I was the fine scholar

I was always

doing fine

"the hypomanic episodes themselves do not cause impairment

*the impairment results from the **Major depressive disadvantage**"*

October

I hated the American Psychiatric Association, when I opened the *Diagnostic and Statistical Manual of Mental Disorders* (2013) that I borrowed from a friend and read myself on its pages. It was like psychiatrists had written the book while watching me in my apartment while I was *"depressed, sad, empty, hopeless, tearful, fatigued—most of the day, nearly every day—markedly disinterested in any activities or pleasure at all; unable to think, to decide anything, to concentrate—except on recurrent thoughts of death"* (p. 133).

This was not the first time I had been left at low tide, like a boat that cannot perform its function; but in graduate school, there is no time for barnacles to dry out waiting for the water to come back in. One must be always on, always performing, always whittling to become fine enough to pass through that sieve at the end of the semester. It was past midterms, I could see the perforations where I might pass through, they were getting closer, but they also seemed to be shrinking.

Hopeless, I remembered that my psychiatrist had said that I needed to be careful with my caffeine intake. Caffeine can create a hypomanic state, he said. So every day I drank three cups of coffee, then two cans of Red Bull, and then I took a 200 mg caffeine pill. In caffeine-induced hypomania, I could see success again.

I was the top of the world, and

it is better

there

more energy

less sleep

restless sleep

I was better

I was fine

I was fine

I was fine.

November

"Rates of completed suicide are 15-fold those of persons in the general population" (Johnson & Tran, 2007, p. 425).

I was drunk and staring at a bottle of codeine, prescribed for my herniated spinal disc.

I hadn't told the nurse I was severely allergic to it.

My phone rang, but I didn't look.

They called again, but I didn't answer.

The phone rang and rang and rang and it was distracting and I picked up and the woman said she was calling from the Suicide Prevention Partnership because someone was worried about me.

She listened while I talked about how life was unsustainable.

> She said, you need to seek medication.

It will help you manage. You don't only have to rely on yourself. People are here to support you. Your friend, he was worried about you. He called us. He's helping you. People will help you, especially if you ask.

What if he had not been watching so closely?

What if he had not known what to look for?

Life in the middle is better, she said.

[Dis]Advantage

> *"Look: here is Dis," he said, "'and here is the place*
> *Where you must arm yourself with the quality*
> *Of fortitude'" (Alighieri, 1317/1994, p. 365).*

December

My psychiatrist was surprised to see me again. I took his prescription, I took the pills, and I spent 2 weeks in a drug-induced zombie state. I had expected this after reading that "difficulty moving" was the most common of the drug's side effects. Knowing the cause did not make the lethargy any easier.

He had said to take the medication at 10:00 p.m. every night and go to bed.

> I had told him he was crazier than I was. I didn't have time with finals to sleep 8 hours.

He had said he knew I didn't *feel* like I had time to sleep that much, but that graduate school would be easier if I did.

> I told him I felt stoned during the day, and that I could not concentrate on my reading, and that I was using my keyboard as a pillow instead of writing my papers.

He said that there would be an adjustment period, and that I shouldn't be concerned.

> But I was concerned: my final papers were due in 2 weeks
>
> and I was never going to finish them.

When faced with the choice of my mental health via SEROQUEL XR or simu-
lated success via caffeine stimulation, I chose success
    but it was a success that looked a lot like failure.
    At 3:00 a.m. on the last day of the semester
    I was throwing up in the bathroom at IHOP
    from drinking a half-gallon of coffee
    to try
    to finish   something
    something I couldn't concentrate on.
    an assignment I should have started in November
    when I could not pull myself out of bed.

THE MIDDLE

When faced with times in our lives when we think we have to choose between
mental health and success, we should aim instead for balance. I do not suggest,
here, that balance is easy. When we are the types with a drive to succeed, we create goals that have paths on which we must sometimes put our mental health at
risk. But we might find balance if we acknowledge that we live in this world in
our towns and on our campuses with hundreds of thousands of millions of other
people. The human factor. We should not feel like we are in this alone.

    Although Johnson and Tran (2007) spoke specifically of persons with bipolar
disorder, the conclusion to their article recommends seeking outside support to
help manage delicate and shifting feelings of self-confidence. I believe these ideas
can be applied universally, especially in graduate school, when we are constantly
stacking ourselves in comparison to our peers. They say:

> As persons begin to recognize how much confidence can vary over time, it becomes easier
> to institute strategies for evaluating the validity of cognitive beliefs about the self. Strategies
> such as asking close others for input about ideas can be accepted more easily once the basic
> fragility of self-evaluations can be shown. (p. 431)

The most important cognitive beliefs about the self that we must question are the
ones that say, "I can do this alone," and "I don't need help." Those are the beliefs
that we will continue to repeat to ourselves over

    and over

    and over

    until we are fragile

    until they have driven us to our breaking point.

When you arrive at your university, I urge you to search the website, or contact student services, and find out what mental health services are offered. Hopefully, at minimum, there should be a number available for a crisis prevention hotline (like the one my friend called for me). We might hope, though, that as American society and the American healthcare system continues to speak more openly about mental health, there might also be a handful of other resources available. My university has psychiatric services with medical counseling and ADHD screening, and therapeutic counseling services that include walk-in appointments, drug and alcohol treatment, and behavioral health services. But until universities require mental health check-ups as rigorously as they require immunizations, you must do the work to seek out these services yourself.

Find out how much of the cost of a mental health visit is covered by your insurance.

If nothing is covered, find a different insurance company.

Start to budget for co-pays the same way you budget for groceries, dinners out, and beers with your cohort.

If the bureaucracy of the mental health network seems daunting (and it can be, to jump through the hoops of the American health insurance system), remember that you are in a program where you sit in class or lab next to other human beings, and that other human beings also teach the lectures and seminars. My experience with my professors and peers has been that having an honest conversation about mental health leads to shared empathy, stories, and advice. After all, personal lives affect academic performance, and so bringing the personal into the advising conversation should be as accepted as asking for input about research and publications. In graduate school, these people must be the "close others" to whom Johnson and Tran (2007) referred, especially if your friends and family cannot understand or do not want to understand why you sacrifice so much for another diploma on your wall and a few more lines on your curriculum vitae.

But we should be honest and kind in our self-evaluations about our abilities, our mental health, and how thin we can be stretched, for sometimes that extra line on the CV may represent our breaking point. Our honesty and self-evaluations will help open our eyes to the tremendous network full of people that we can rely on for input rather than for competition. When I viewed graduate school through the dichotomy of success versus failure, I was forced to look at faculty members as hard metal sieves who impart only either success or failure, and I was forced to look at my peers as competition, and I was forced to hold myself to unreasonable standards of performance. And though academia does hold very real standards of success and competition, the academy is also made up of very real human beings.

However, if you are not ready to rely on these other human beings or experience the relief that comes from an hour of talking with an objective stranger, then, at the very least, be rigorous in your practices of self-care. Start right now. Write down three activities that you can do in less than 30 minutes that make you feel calm/more centered/happy (here's mine: Making the bed. Reading a few pages of something not related to school. Taking a bath). Tape this piece of paper to the wall above your computer, and actually *do* these things while you are studying for tests, writing papers, or when you get home from a long experiment in the lab.

And, lastly, try to keep an eye out for those around you. In high-achieving students, like those of us who seek out graduate studies, mental health problems are sometimes hard to see. Form study groups or reading clubs, but especially know the warning signs of suicide. If someone talks frequently about death, or expresses self-loathing, or exhibits self-destructive behavior, then speak up. Ask them if they have considered getting help, or how you can support them. And if somebody asks you these questions, thank them. If we constantly disguise our struggles in performances of success, we put ourselves at risk. Struggling with the demands of graduate school is normal. Considering suicide should not be, so talking about mental health needs to be.

REFERENCES

Alighieri, D. (1994). *The inferno* (R. Pinsky, Trans.). New York, NY: Farrar, Straus, and Giroux (Original work published 1317)

American Psychiatric Association. (2013). *Diagnostic and statistical manual of mental* (5th ed.). Washington, DC: Author.

AstraZeneca. (2013). *SEROQUEL XR (quetiapine fumarate): Medication guide.* Retrieved from http://www.fda.gov/downloads/Drugs/DrugSafety/UCM194582.pdf

Johnson, S., & Tran, T. (2007). Bipolar disorder: What can psychotherapists learn from the cognitive research? *Journal of Clinical Psychology: In Session, 63*(5), 425–432.

CHAPTER THIRTEEN

Navigating Traditional Graduate Programs as a Non-Traditional Student

CHRISTOPHER A. HUFF

INTRODUCTION

Few things are more challenging or rewarding than making it to the end of a doctoral program. It is the ultimate prize. Keep your eyes on it as you begin your graduate school journey because many obstacles lurk on the path to that prize, hoping to trip you up. Difficult professors, financial worries, impossible deadlines, ignored friendships: it's likely every graduate student will stumble over these bumps in the road. For non-traditional students, those with additional responsibilities—families, mortgages, aging bodies that can't bounce back from hangovers quite as quickly—these issues loom even larger. But do not despair. Success awaits the well-prepared and persistent traveller.

At least part of what follows will be useful to anyone wanting to enrol full time in a humanities doctoral program, but it is aimed most directly at non-traditional graduate students. No really useful definition of the term "non-traditional student" exists, and even in my limited experience of attending one graduate program at one university, I would be hard-pressed to come up with one. I've known all kinds of non-traditional students—divorcees in their 40s, young men just hitting their mid-20s with a spouse and several children, even independently wealthy people well past retirement age who arrive to class discussions of Marxism in late-model Porsches. Any attempt to address the concerns of such a varied group would verge on the futile. Instead, I will speak to what I consider the group most likely to be seeking out the advice this chapter offers: someone in their 30s and 40s who is financially independent from his oe her parents (but not independently wealthy); a person with a family, or who may be single but not ruling out acquiring a spouse and children before graduating; and someone who has committed themselves to pursuing a doctoral degree in hopes of changing his or her career path. This was me when I started graduate school more than a decade ago.

This chapter will discuss some basic issues you should consider in reaching a decision about entering graduate school as a non-traditional student. While you obviously have the desire to pursue a doctoral degree (why else would you be reading this book?), it is equally important to figure out if you possess what it takes to succeed. Acquiring a doctoral degree will consume somewhere between 5 and 10 years of your life, and while it has the potential to be the best experience of your life it also holds out the possibility for the exact opposite. Much like taking a cross-country car trip with small children, you need to ask a lot of questions, plan thoroughly, and really consider if this is the best method for reaching your destination.

IT'S JOB TRAINING, BUT WHAT KIND AND FOR WHAT JOB?

During graduate school orientation my department head emphasized that, above all else, graduate school is *job training*. We understood this fact, of course, but did not really grasp at the time how it translated into the realities of the current-day academic job market. We dreamed, as you may, of securing a full-time, tenure-track position as a college professor. It is an enticing dream. Many graduate students envision themselves strolling across the leaf-covered quadrangle of some small New England liberal arts college in early fall, trailed by inquisitive undergraduates. Or, perhaps, for the more research-minded, they see themselves holding court with talented graduate students in a coffeehouse just off the campus of a major university, discussing the arguments in their most recent prizewinning book. These are obtainable goals. Increasingly, though, they are obtainable in the same way that an actor can obtain an Oscar or a baseball player can secure a spot in the starting line-up of the Philadelphia Phillies.

The current realities of American higher education have created what can be called harsh hiring and working conditions. The number of tenure track positions has dwindled as colleges and universities grow increasingly dependent on contingent faculty—people with terminal degrees in their fields who are hired on a semester or yearly basis. They may teach a full-time course load at one school, or cobble together a full-time schedule by working at more than one school at a time. These faculty members make on average about $3000 per three credit hour course (June & Newman, 2013). Recent surveys have shown that contingent faculty comprises 76% of the college instructor appointments, and while these professors probably do spend time in coffeehouses, they are likely just running in to grab a cup to drink on the ride across town for their afternoon survey lecture (American Association of University Professors, 2015).

Improving the Job Placement Odds

These are daunting facts but there are ways to work the graduate school system in your favor to avoid this result. First, apply to programs that have strong records of getting students tenure-track jobs. In the subject area of history, for example, a 2015 study concluded that eight schools produce half of all history professors (Warner & Clauset, 2015). Set your sights on those programs. Or, if you already have a solid understanding of what specific area in your field you want to study, your program search should center on finding a faculty advisor that is at the top of that specialty. Even though you may not be attending the most prestigious university, being trained by an acknowledged expert will improve your chances of acquiring a tenure track position. The concept of mentorship plays a major role in the graduate school landscape, and having the right mentor can improve greatly your attractiveness to hiring committees. If neither of these approaches produces a favorable result, seriously consider entering a respectable Master of Arts program as a gateway to a better program. I know several people who completed an MA in an unranked program and transferred to top tier and Ivy League universities for their doctorate.

You may also want to consider a non-academic career. In the humanities, this may be your best option for obtaining permanent, well-compensated employment in a part of the country where you want to live. This decision can make you a lone wolf in graduate school, but hey, if you are willing to change career paths at this point, you are already working outside the pack. A growing number of higher education pundits encourage the pursuit of a career outside the academy as a viable and respectable goal of graduate education. At the moment, though, they are definitely the minority voice. Graduate students regularly post to message boards about how advisors or other faculty members look poorly upon the decision to seek this kind of work. In the end, however, this is your journey, not theirs, so consider all the factors when deciding what works best for you.

MONEY, IT'S A DRAG

The financial challenges of completing graduate training can prove the most complex and difficult to conquer. You may have heard, as I did when I was applying to programs, that if you have to pay to go to graduate school, you are doing something wrong. After all, don't graduate programs financially support their students? Well, yes and no. Any decent program will provide some kind of stipend or assistantship to its students (and usually comes with a tuition waiver). How you acquire these funds, how much you receive, and for how long, can vary greatly. In general, these amounts are fairly small, have time limits attached to them, and almost certainly do not cover all the financial needs of non-traditional students. The calculation of funding by departments is still based on the notion that new graduate students are coming right out of an undergraduate program, have no debt or family obligations, and can easily accept an austere lifestyle. Funding might cover reasonable rent payments and the most basic living expenses, but not much else. In addition, such arrangements usually have time limits that expire around the 5-year mark. Given that the average length of time to completion of a humanities doctoral program is 9 years, this will leave you looking for sources of income during the years in which you need to focus most on researching and writing your dissertation.

The easiest financial course, obviously, lies in coming to graduate school debt-free and with minimal financial obligations. The standard good advice applies: pay off the credit cards and car loans. Have some kind of savings available for emergencies, unforeseen necessities or the occasional luxury. Non-traditional students, however, are often coming in without the possibility of a clean slate. You are changing careers by going to graduate school, which means you had a career (or at least a decent-paying job) before making the decision to return to school. You built a financial life on a level of income that will, in all likelihood, be reduced greatly by becoming a student. It will be difficult to alter your financial situation to this new reality without making significant sacrifices.

These sacrifices will likely affect how you view yourself and what you are doing. More than anything else, it was the changes to my financial situation that made me question if I had made the right choice. At a time when I should have been building savings, thinking about retirement accounts, and otherwise enjoying the fruits of my labors, I instead acquired new debt, took longer to pay off existing debt, owned the same car for far longer than I ever planned, and made tough choices constantly about how to spend my (very) limited disposable income. I had a house, a wife, and a young child, so living like a monk in a bare studio apartment and toughing it out was not an option. Extended vacations were replaced by short weekends closer to home. Dinner and a movie became dinner OR a movie. In the last 2 years of graduate school, I turned off cable TV and replaced it with inexpensive streaming video services. By doing some or all of these things, it may feel like you are not moving forward in your life. But, that will simply not be true. You will be completing course requirements, getting articles published, presenting at conferences, and researching your dissertation. You will be moving closer to graduation every day. These financial struggles also kept me mindful of why I went back to school in the first place. I wanted to make a qualitative, not quantitative, change to my life. I am far happier now because of the work I am doing, not because of how much I am being compensated for it.

TIME MANAGEMENT

Graduate school is a massive time commitment; there is no way around this fact. The number of hours you will commit daily to succeeding in graduate school is far larger than that required at the undergraduate level, and, unless you are currently working a couple of full-time jobs, much greater than your current work obligations. Most of this comes from understanding that *there is always more work to do*. You will never be caught up or finished. At least not in a way that makes you think, "Hey, I can take a few guilt-free weeks off and think about something else." It is not going to happen. From the moment you start there will always be the next book to read, the next paper to write, the next research trip to plan, the next conference to apply to, the next fellowship proposal to submit, and, of course, grading, grading, and more grading. This experience has its positive aspects. It is, after all, why you wanted to attend grad school in the first place—it is how a life dedicated to mind actually works. And it is a fascinating and exciting experience. You are constantly engaging new topics, events, ideas, and arguments. You will be as submerged as you will ever be in the pure pursuit of knowledge, and, even more thrilling, figuring out your place in it.

Building a CV

Looking at it from a more practical perspective, you have no choice but to do these things. Given the state of the academic job market you **must** build as strong a CV (curriculum vitae—the academic term for resume) as you can. The elements that make a strong CV are not the same elements needed to complete your graduation requirements. You finish grad school by taking courses, passing qualifying examinations and writing a dissertation. You get a job by presenting at conferences, publishing articles in peer-reviewed journals, winning research grants, and, one can hope, receiving a few awards for your work along the way. You have taken on, in effect, two more-than-full-time jobs.

It's a life that leaves room for little else. It encourages an ascetic lifestyle, but for the non-traditional student it creates a unique set of challenges since the ascetic lifestyle is not an option. You may have familial obligations of some kind—a spouse/significant other, perhaps a child or two. At the very least, you will have long-term friendships you want to maintain. Graduate school can severely damage or destroy these relationships if you are not careful. It's the most jealous of mistresses—think Glenn Close in *Fatal Attraction*—and, if you let it, it will stalk you night and day. Please, do not let this happen to you. I entered graduate school with a wife and left it with the same wife and a daughter. While I'm very proud of what I accomplished in my graduate career I am far more pleased that by the end I still had a great relationship with my family.

Suggested Strategies

Success in this area will result from adopting two strategies for managing your time. Most importantly, figure out the difference between what you *need* to do and what you *want* to do. You will be presented with the opportunity to participate in a wide variety of extracurricular events from the departmental level on up. There will be lectures by visiting scholars, workshops on interesting topics, various brown bag lunch discussions—the list goes on. You will be tempted to attend each of these events. Who wouldn't want to see an award-winning author or a Nobel Prize winner speak? I certainly did. By foregoing many of these events, though, you can keep a focus on what needs to get done—preparing for class discussions, writing essays, conducting research, and completing TA duties.

Making these choices (and they can be tough ones) will help put into play the second strategy. I not only wanted to have time for my wife (and later, child) but I wanted to make sure the time I spent with them mattered. That long list of never-ending tasks mentioned above can consume your every thought. Given the reduction in the amount of time you can spend with your family, the worst thing you can do to them is be there physically but not mentally. Even worse, it's possible to grow resentful of how they are taking you away from what you think you need to do. I know, I know—you swear this will not happen to you, but it can, and possibly will. You can avoid this trap by intentionally dedicating time to your family and friends and treating that time as sacred and inviolate. It will feel a bit artificial at first—"hey honey, let's do nights out on Friday and go to the park or the zoo on Sunday afternoons and have the Millers over three Saturdays from now." So much gets thrown at you in grad school that it will be easy to not follow your well-planned-out-but-limited social schedule. DON'T DO IT. Stick to your timetable—it's too important. In a short while you will view these times as a refuge and haven. I looked forward to talking about something other than cross-cultural contact in Northern Africa. A few hours in the world of a 2-year-old serves as a fantastic break from writing essays about Michel Foucault. These times remind you that a big and interesting world exists outside of grad school.

THE FRIENDS AND FAMILY PLAN

Sometime around the third year in grad school, I began wishing fervently that I could find a short and firm way of telling my family and friends to stop asking me exactly what I had to do to graduate and get a job. Something along the lines of *Fight Club:* "The first rule of me being in grad school is you not asking me about grad school." Because, bless their hearts, they do mean well, but they will likely never wrap their heads around what you have to do. In all fairness, getting a doctoral degree is very different from how most people understand higher education. To your family and friends, college means passing a set number of classes in a small window of time. This, of course, is definitely NOT what you do to get a PhD. You will likely have some version of this conversation over and over and over again:

"So how is grad school going?"

"Great! I'm almost done with my coursework."

"So then you are almost ready to graduate?"

"Well, no. Then I have to take qualifying exams. That's about six months to a year."

"Then you will be done?"

"Nope—after that I have to write a dissertation proposal and have it approved by a committee of professors—"

"—Well, that can't tak—"

"—followed by three to five years of researching and writing the actual dissertation."

"And THEN you will graduate?"

"Yes! Well, assuming my committee approves my dissertation."

"I thought they did that already."

"No. They approved the plan for my dissertation—now they have to approve the dissertation itself."

"Oh. Look! It's Aunt Kathy! I haven't spoken to her in ages. Excuse me."

Non-traditional students can also look forward to the possibility that some people in their lives may look down on them for going back to school. After all, you already went to college. You have a job. What is wrong with you for throwing all that away to become a COLLEGE STUDENT again? What kind of Vince Vaughn-esque man-child are you trying to be? I hope you will not encounter any of these folks. Then again, you might. I had a relative who, every time I talked to him during my entire grad school career, would ask in the same semi-joking manner if I was still "refusing to be a productive member of society and living off the government." I'm still not sure how he arrived at that interpretation. Sadly, I have no better advice on how to deal with these things other than to grin and bear it. Be patient with them. These folks will be an important, if not always understanding, part of your support network. Also, these are the same people who will have to suffer politely through your 20-minute answer to the question, "So what is your dissertation about anyway?"

CONCLUSION

As a non-traditional student you have more concerns than most. From money to family to stretching yourself ever thinner to meet the numerous demands placed on your time, grad school will likely be the greatest challenge you have ever taken on. Is it worth it? That's for you to decide. This chapter provides a starting point as you begin thinking about attending graduate school, but I encourage you to dig deeper. Contact professors in your field of interest and e-mail grad students at programs you find attractive. Ask them about how the general issues raised above apply to your specific situation. While you cannot plan for every possibility or do enough to avoid all obstacles, your chances of success in grad school as a non-traditional student will be greatly improved by doing as much research and thinking as you can before you step into that first seminar room. I wish you the best.

REFERENCES

American Association of University Professors. (2015). *Background facts on contingent faculty.* Retrieved from http://www.aaup.org/issues/contingency/background-facts

June, A., & Newman, J. (2013, January 4). *Adjunct project reveals wide range in pay.* Retrieved from http://chronicle.com/article/Adjunct-Project-Shows-Wide/136439/

Warner, J., & Clauset, A. (2015, February 23). *The academy's dirty secret.* Retrieved from http://www.slate.com/articles/life/education/2015/02/university_hiring_if_you_didn_t_get_your_ph_d_at_an_elite_university_good.html

PART FOUR

Maintaining Wellness: Looking After You

CHAPTER FOURTEEN

The Student's Practical Guide to Not Losing Your Soul

NICHOLAS R. WERSE AND B. J. PARKER

INTRODUCTION

Recently a colleague of ours—we'll call her Sarah—told me that she was completely out of gas. Her 2-and-a-half years of working on her dissertation produced a half-finished manuscript that left her with little love for the material. In the conversation she told me that the only reason she was finishing was sheer pride. What happened? It's probably safe to say that when someone decides to start graduate school, the individual does so because he or she has a passion for the material—it's certainly not for the money. So what happened to Sarah and the countless others who confess similar words? Graduate education is a rewarding, yet intense and demanding period of life that, when left unchecked, can grow into a monster.

After completing our respective master's degrees in the field of religion, we both pursued doctoral work at a research institution in the field of religious studies. After over seven years of graduate-level education, having completed coursework, presented and published academic papers, and maintained some semblance of health, we find ourselves in the position of talking to incoming students as well as participating in interdisciplinary reading groups that discuss the formation of scholars. After years of confronting the many ways that graduate school can rob students of the joys of life, we find ourselves increasingly offering the same tips to eager young scholars embarking upon their graduate journey. In this chapter we not only discuss why we have found graduate school to be a taxing undertaking, but we also introduce the six practices that we have found most helpful for maintaining balance in the heart of the storm. In short, we offer what has become our practical guide to not losing your soul in graduate school.

COUNTING THE COSTS OF GRADUATE EDUCATION

For all the wonderful ways that graduate education can form an individual, it can also have detrimental effects. Anyone reading this chapter is likely familiar with the time that graduate programs require of students; a commitment of 5 to 10 years of sustained focus could be the entry fee. For most of those years, students' work-weeks fluctuate between 50 to 80 hours (or more). A 60-hour workweek amounts to five 12-hour days or six 10-hour days—neither of which leads to long-term health. We fill the purported school "breaks" of winter and summer with writing, editing, and/or preparation for comprehensive exams. Not only does graduate education make enormous demands on a student's time, but the savvy student also looks for opportunities for professional development through committees, conferences, and workshops. On top of these commitments, graduate students often need to supplement their meager stipends through adjunct teaching. Graduate education can be a consuming undertaking.

In addition to time slipping away, graduate students often feel a strong sense of pressure. A seminar always looms with its requisite negotiation of pedantry. Once a student feels free of the stress of a seminar meeting, he or she has to think about the research paper that will soon be due. "What will the professor think of my idea?" "Will this professor still want to direct my dissertation after this paper?" "Can they kick me out for one bad paper?" When not worrying about seminars or seminar papers, comprehensive exams always loom on the horizon and exert their fair share of stress on the already saturated mind. Once one navigates the pressure of exams, a brilliant dissertation and stellar teaching evaluations are all that separate the graduate student from the one job for which 20 are applying. Higher education exerts short-term and long-term stress on the student. We might reframe this type of pressure as "chronic stress."

Individuals who dare to brave this gauntlet of stress must also consider the impact upon the long-term well-being of themselves and those around them. How does chronic stress impact one's love of a subject—or love of anything, for that matter? And what of friendships, marriages, extended families, and faith communities? When one feeds the beast of success at any cost, we would argue that not much good results. In light of this tale of woe, the following tips are six ways a graduate student can reorient throughout the process of higher education.

Tip 1: Forbidden Sacrifices on the Altar of Graduate Student Success

We students joke about sacrificing our social amenability on the altar of graduate student success. It only takes a few short months barricaded in the dark recesses of our institutional library before we find ourselves wading through an incomprehensible web of unnecessary technical argot in a desperate attempt to find the necessary colloquialism with which to order a hamburger at our favorite local eatery. The truth is that graduate school success requires great sacrifice. The danger, however, is that if we are not intentional about what we are and *are not* willing to sacrifice, then the demands of graduate school may quickly begin stealing treasured parts of our lives when we are not looking. The quest to write that publishable paper can easily veil the fact that we have not talked to our significant other about anything other than the stresses of our glorious graduate student enterprise to master some small piece of the universe. In the heart of the semester, we may become so consumed with keeping up with our coursework that we can easily forget to have tea parties with our daughter, play with our puppy, or attend a local community art fair. If we are not cognizant, graduate school may steal some of the moments we cherish most in our everyday lives without us even noticing.

For this reason, one of the first practical tips we give to incoming graduate students is to intentionally decide at the beginning of your program what you are and *are not* willing to sacrifice for graduate school. Sacrifices will have to be made, so decide early which sacrifices are forbidden upon your altar. Label them anathema; desecrations that you will not allow to anything you consider holy in your life! Such intentionality may seem simple, but it enables us to remain cognizant of what we lose during our tenure as bibliophilic recluses. Such cognizance keeps us vigilant against losing the very things we cherish the most. We decided, for example, that we were willing to sacrifice playing recreational sports; but we were not willing to sacrifice our spousal relationships. We, of course, have occasionally participated in pick-up basketball games; but when the demands of school summon our immediate obedience, these games are willingly laid at the foot of the altar. We have intentionally decided, however, that no matter how bad the semester gets, no thesis, dissertation, or study group will take priority over designated family dinners.

This list of acceptable sacrifices may have to be revisited periodically to make necessary adjustments. We may get through our first year of coursework and conclude that we are grumpy curmudgeons worthy of our own Internet meme franchise and that we should incorporate more time for creative outlets before an impersonation of us requires little more than a series of grunts and the "evil eye" we give when the coffee pot is empty. This list may be something we have to consider with the help of other important people in our lives. Our decision to attend graduate school often affects those closest to us. Spouses and children should have a voice in deciding how our sacrifices will impact their lives over the next several years.

Tip 2: Create a Schedule and Let the Schedule Protect You

Whether students ask us about succeeding in publishing, coursework, or maintaining their extra-curricular commitments, the advice is always the same: "Create a schedule and let the schedule protect you." Whether it is a daily planner, a smart phone app, or a tattoo on your forehead, anytime you want to protect a commitment from numerous demands on your time, a written schedule can help.

Calculate how much time you will devote to your school-related responsibilities and schedule clearly demarcated time blocks for them in your week. This task necessitates clearly communicating with your professors about the temporal expectations for course preparation and how many hours a particular assistantship will require. Thus, if your assistantship requires 10 hours per week, then schedule what 10 hours you will devote to those responsibilities. Decide what days and times you will devote to preparing for what classes. Setting this schedule will enable you to control how many hours per week are devoted to school, and thus protect the hours you want to devote elsewhere.

Enshrine those aforementioned commitments that you are not willing to sacrifice on the altar of graduate student success in your schedule. Write in the regularly reoccurring times when you will play baseball with your son, or cook a family dinner. If you want to maintain certain friendships, then write in times for *non-academic* lunch appointments. On any given month, we will have a recreational function on the calendar and the name of a friend we are attending with.

Let the schedule protect you. When we schedule 15 hours per week to prepare for one seminar, if we do not complete the required preparations, then we simply don't finish for that week. We gave it all of the time that we were willing to give and now we must move on in order to fulfill our other commitments, including those extra-curricular ones. There have been times when both of us have told a professor that we did not complete the reading because it exceeded our allotted time for course preparation. When we go to the library for a scheduled time of research and writing, we do not respond to e-mails for our assistantships. Keeping each of the school-related responsibilities within their scheduled times enables us to carefully control the amount of time devoted to school and thus prevent the (seemingly unrealistic) demands of graduate school from stealing time away from our other valued commitments. Strictly maintaining the temporal limits on school-related activities will prevent you from suddenly looking up from your peaceful study only to shout "thief!" out the window as you watch your academic responsibilities running down the street with that half-finished scarf that in some incarnation of its existence was supposed to be Aunt Wilma's Christmas gift.

Tip 3: Don't Talk Shop Off the Clock

Once you've enshrined the things you value most in your schedule and have successfully beaten back the beast of your own over-achieving personality, you will have to master perhaps the hardest skill of the guild: "don't talk shop off the clock." It is hard for a graduate student to get off the clock. When we spend close to 80 hours per week working on a thesis, it is difficult to transition our minds into thinking about anything else. Yet learning to leave school-related matters at school is crucial to safeguarding our extra-curricular values. This practice keeps the stresses of school from invading (and potentially defiling) other life-giving extra-curricular activities. For the record, we are really bad at this. It generally takes a spouse to notify us of when we transgress this sacred precept. Yet whether we are gathering with our academic colleagues for drinks, or our extended family for Thanksgiving, it is important to be able to converse on topics other than school. And here is another plus: being able to talk about something other than your work contributes to the perception of amenability, and being a pleasant person to work with is still an important factor in finding employment.

To be fair, there are times when friends and family genuinely want to know about your studies. We should not, however, mistake Aunt Wilma's casual inquiry over dinner as an invitation for an overly dramatic monologue on the glories of our half-written esoteric dissertations. In general, we advise students to have a 20–30-second snapshot of their thesis, or semesterly adventures. Aunt Wilma may of course inquire further about something we say, but we want to intentionally pause often so as to let her drive the conversation forward with her questions, rather than be run over by our academic ambitions and dragged the rest of the way through dinner like Coke cans on the back of a newlywed's Prius.

Tip 4: Foster Friendships Outside of School

Develop friendships outside of school. Friendships outside of our typical circles can be regenerative on some of the deepest levels. When we are surrounded by people like ourselves (in our case, whose minds constantly analyze the rhetorical strength of an argument and begin thinking of ways to either demolish or bolster it), we can quickly become poor conversation partners and wretched friends. When sitting down for a cup of coffee, who really wants to hear a critical analysis of the way in which the oppressive spatial semiotics of the coffee shop require a thoroughgoing liberative remodeling? Deep friendships can lead us out of the labyrinth of academia and back into the sunlight of reality.

When you spend all of your time holed up in the library reading and thinking about the contours of Enlightenment Philosophy applied to Post-Deconstructionist furniture-making in newly urbanized rural communities you can quickly morph into someone who is, well, barely human. Friends remind us that playing a game of basketball can be a balm. A night spent with friends, food, and drink can do more to restore sanity and rejuvenate the soul than any academic accomplishment. Being with friends forces us to be vulnerable and to value others—something that critiquing secondary literature typically prohibits.

The importance of friendships causes us to enshrine time with those we call friends on a regular basis. Short of the sacrosanct time with spouses, we work to ensure that we spend the occasional afternoon hiking with friends or evening playing board games such as Carcassonne. While the obligations of the semester ebb and flow, restricting our ability to be with friends, Wednesday Pub Night maintains a central place in our weekly schedule.

Tip 5: Find a Hobby Outside of School

When making decisions about what to cut during a season of chronic stress, we often set our hobbies on the chopping block first. We suggest, however, that doing so might be one of the worst decisions a graduate student can make. Though it is easy to forget amidst the piles of papers to grade, books to read, and committee responsibilities to fulfill, we are not the sum of what we produce. Hobbies remind us of this fact. When you feel the dirt under your feet and even breathing as you run along a 5k trail and look out at a quiet river, you can slide back into rhythms that are much bigger than your anxieties. When you feel the buttery texture of cerulean blue glide across a canvas or your hands on the keys of a piano, you can viscerally remember who you are. Hobbies work to re-member us. Spending time doing things we love relaxes us, restores us, and enables us to breathe. When we go back to our formal work, we often have more vigor, creativity, and excitement.

How do we practically take time for hobbies amidst an already crowded and stressful semester? We have found three strategies helpful. First, enjoy your hobby in small chunks of time. Few people work well through long, sustained blocks of time. We like to work for 45 minutes to an hour and then take a 10-minute break during which we might pick up a guitar or work on a sketch. Second, we have found that 30 minutes to an hour every other day can also be a great way to block off time to do something we love. Third, just like we guard our time with our spouses, we also enshrine the time we have set aside for woodworking or yoga. There will *always* be more academic work to do. More does not equal a better you.

Tip 6: Consistently Revisit Your Vocation

For those of us who undertake a master's degree (or two!) before beginning a PhD, graduate school can easily encompass a decade of life. The years that we devote to study not only reflect our transition from student to teacher/scholar, but they also encompass basic life changes. Many begin graduate school close on the heels of bachelor's degrees. Within this period of life, many move to different cities, marry, have children, learn to negotiate family dynamics, and sometimes divorce. Those who come to graduate school later in life still negotiate many of the same changes. Taken together, these sorts of fluctuations in life are simultaneously unpredictable and definitive. In light of the transitions that take place during graduate education, the descriptor "formation" certainly applies. Because graduate school functions as an extended period of both reflection and formation we argue that we need to consistently revisit what we perceive to be our vocation.

Vocation in the classical sense refers to a summons or call to something. Whether it be curiosity, fascination, the guidance of a mentor or the admiration of a role model, something compels us into the discipline for a purpose. When we begin graduate school, we often have a strong sense of vocation—we want to be a professor of English literature, or figure painting, or chemistry. We want to study and steward the material we love, shape young minds, and research cutting-edge ideas in our field; and so we enter a graduate degree program in our respective area. The years that follow are by design intense. They often affirm *or* negate what we perceive to be our vocations. Both of these are invaluable outcomes.

One of our colleagues, we'll call her Beth, has found that the process of graduate school has affirmed what she perceives to be her vocation in a very deep way. She finds that her work on Shakespeare enlivens her. Prelims were a time of celebration in that she was able to devote large amounts of time to reading and thinking about ideas that made her live more intensely. Beth's publishing has also affirmed her sense of calling as a scholar. Having experienced both rejections and acceptances, Beth's research and publication reflect more her passion than her need to succeed. Finally, her classroom experiences have also affirmed her role as teacher. The beautiful teaching moments that occur on a regular basis remind her that she loves introducing people to great literature.

Not everyone's experience in graduate school, however, mirrors that of Beth. Some find that graduate education perpetually frustrates and challenges their conception of their vocation. In *Let Your Life Speak: Listening for the Voice of Vocation*, Parker Palmer (2000) recounted how his initial attempts to line up the lofty ideals he received from his PhD with his vocation led him to a state of deep depression and burnout. After 5 years of living out ideals that did not fit with what he called his "native way of being in the world," Palmer moved to a Quaker community where he learned to quietly listen to his motivations, fears, and hopes in the process of discerning his vocation as teacher and not as activist. He offered the following reflection:

> Vocation does not come from willfulness. It comes from listening. I must listen to my life and try to understand what it is truly about—quite apart from what I would like it to be

about—or my life will never represent anything real in the world, no matter how earnest my intentions. (p. 4)

Though we might not retreat to a Quaker community, we would all do well to incorporate vocational reflection into our lives. The intense and formative process that is graduate education offers us ample opportunity to listen to our lives and clarify our vocation. We encourage incoming students to make such reflection a regular part of life. Self-discovery always benefits the individual. While discovering one's vocational identity as artist or counselor during a research degree in chemistry might be a complicated process, ignoring this identity poses far more dangers than embracing it.

CONCLUSION

This survival guide grew out of years of conversations as we reflected upon the times when we most succeeded in graduate school, and the times when we barely survived. We are fortunate to be a part of an interdisciplinary community on our campus, enabling us to discuss these issues with colleagues from other fields of study. Over the years our scattered thoughts have coalesced into these six tips, which really revolve around two principles. The first principle is being intentional about how our time is spent. To this end, enshrining a set schedule on a calendar and letting that calendar protect our commitments (whether they be hobbies, friends, or anything else we refuse to sacrifice) has been immensely helpful. The second principle involves intentionally taking time to reflect upon our graduate student experience. This reflection might happen once per year or once per month. In either case, it is important to intentionally reflect upon the impact of our graduate school experience upon our lives and our sense of vocation. Intentional self-reflection has not only enabled us to keep our fingers on the pulse of the motivations driving us in the academy, but it has also allowed us to gauge what adjustments need to be made in our regular schedules and weekly routines to ensure that graduate school remains a truly enjoyable experience.

REFERENCE

Palmer, P. J. (2000). *Let your life speak: Listening for the voice of vocation.* San Francisco, CA: Jossey-Bass.

CHAPTER FIFTEEN

Hooker Boots and Edgar Allan Poe

Finding Inspiration in Grad School

TABATHA HOFFMEYER

INTRODUCTION

"True, nervous, very, very dreadfully nervous I had been and am; but why will you say that I am mad?"

This is the introduction to Poe's macabre short story "The Telltale Heart." I performed a one-act for a school competition many years ago and every time that I get myself into a particularly stressful situation these words repeat themselves over and over in my head. Don't worry, there's no dead body hidden in my wall. I'm talking about grad school, and I promise that all of my professors are alive and accounted for. If you are reading this, you are either contemplating starting grad school or you've already enrolled. You may be wondering how you can possibly juggle the madness of writing papers, work a full-time job, and even take care of three kids. Lucky for you, I've been there and survived (many times by the skin of my teeth) and it was one of the most challenging and satisfying things that I've ever done.

The Poe quote surfaced once again as I lamented over how I was going to let down my hair and get into my comfort zone while writing this chapter. I wanted to be able to tap into the emotional highs and lows that I was experiencing along the way as well as open up to you in a way that seems most natural to me, so I decided to take a trip through social media memory lane. Social media provide me a way to momentarily escape from the stress. When you're up at 3:00 a.m. and you begin hallucinating from exhaustion, taking a quiz that will definitively let you know which '80s hunky Hollywood bad boy is your ultimate soul mate may just be the thing that coaxes you off the ledge.

I learned several things about myself as I was reviewing my past. Sarcastic humor is on the top of my list of coping mechanisms; I may need to ease back on the drinking a tad; and the best feeling in the world is being curled up in bed at the end of a long, exhausting day. In this chapter I invite you to crawl in with me, pour yourself a drink, and relax as we hop back through time and explore what kept me sane, what pushed me to my limits, and what I did to motivate myself to keep trudging on. Along with sharing my "bed" with you, I will share insight into the importance of getting involved and creating relationships that will benefit you academically and emotionally. I will talk about ways to cope with one of the commonest adversaries, self-doubt. And I will challenge you to find what I refer to as my "Erik," the reason that I am here today, encouraging you to take that giant leap and follow your passion.

> Status Update: It seems I didn't get the memo about wearing hooker boots and short shorts to class today. I guess I'm going to have put a little more effort at my hot yoga class if I'm going to get a proper education. Don't get me wrong, I have quite the extensive collection of hooker boots but I reserve them for more appropriate occasions like parent teacher conferences and charity fundraisers. While baring your butt cheeks in front of a professor who taught Moses how to play patty cake is entertaining enough, I would prefer to get through this 97-page PowerPoint on Comparison of Attributes of Educational Philosophies so I can go home and get naked in my Snuggie with a bottle of Merlot.

You may find it a bit ironic that I am asking you to jump into bed with me after my introductory status update, but beyond my beautiful face and sparkly personality, I do have much more to offer you than the aforementioned Miss Butt Cheeks. I just finished grad school. I have experience. And the best part of it for you is that my experience wasn't always pretty. The odds were certainly not in my favor. Had I been in the Hunger Games I would have been stung by Tracker Jackers, mulled by Mutations, and poisoned by berries before I even volunteered to be a tribute. Even if you haven't seen the movies (I mean, read all of the books), you get the point. Grad school is tough, life is tough, but if you can find your passion and constantly find ways to feed this passion and seek out people and opportunities that will help you become the person that you want to be, it's totally doable. So pour me another glass, move in a little closer, and let's begin. Nothing in "the book" says grad school doesn't have to be fun, or that you can't have fun while getting through it.

MAKE THE MOST OF RELATIONSHIPS

> Status Update: Went out for drinks tonight with the Grad School equivalent of the Breakfast Club. We had the professor, the cougar, the slightly annoying always have a sunny

disposition on life girl…okay, maybe it was more like the Gilligan's Island of Grad School. I figure if we're all going to be stranded on the island together, we better explore each other's strengths and weakness. I suppose you could call me the Captain, not just because I've taken charge of bringing this motley crew together but because I have the perfect pair of knee high pirate boots in my closet that are begging to be worn.

Grad school is not just undergrad classes on steroids. This is a whole new relationship. You will be surrounded by people who share the same passions as you. You can have intelligent experience- and knowledge-based conversations with classmates who will challenge you, encourage you, and titillate the furthest reaches of your gray matter. I'm getting tingly just thinking about it. Chances are, you will be seeing these faces not only throughout the course of your grad work but also in professional settings from here until eternity. Use these people. That may sound a little harsh, but let me explain. Every person that you meet has something to offer. This could be academic advice, it could be emotional support, and they might even help contribute to your physical well-being. I've trained and run races with classmates, I've had mutual counselling sessions with classmates whose situations parallel mine, and I've had late-night research parties at the local bar that resulted in exemplary work and a slight hangover. And don't limit yourself to classmates. Yes—it's okay to befriend your professors as well. Trust me, it's not going to make you uncool. One of the biggest boosts of confidence that I received is when one of my professors asked me if I could come evaluate a situation outside the classroom and give her some advice on how to handle it. I had developed an area of expertise that was exhibited beyond the confines of my own mind, and that's a pretty uplifting thing.

The thing about grad school is that you are most probably not going to have the same opportunities that you had as an undergraduate to socially connect with people. You probably won't be living on campus, you won't be hanging out at frat parties and nailing the title of keg stand queen (well, maybe once, but I got a free t-shirt out of it), or attending sporting events and pep rallies. Chances are you won't even know what your school mascot is, and if you do you would rather have a scholarly debate on what substance could possibly have resulted in the concoction of a mascot with the paws of a cheetah, horns of a buffalo, and face of a Saint Bernard. The point is, make those connections. Get to know people. Grad school can be isolating, you will be turning down invitations to go out with friends (yes, even on Friday nights) because you have a 20-page literature review due by midnight that you have yet to start. Your usual circle may support you, but they won't get it. You will meet people that do. Surround yourself with people that educate you, people that challenge you, and people that inspire you. As a Girl Scout and rather unorthodox troop leader, our little uniform-clad minions would chant the words, "make new friends but keep the old, one is silver and the other gold."

INOCULATE AGAINST SELF-DOUBT AND SHINE!

Status Update: Just got an e-mail from my professor saying, and I quote, "Your final paper was excellent." Now I don't like to brag but the seventeenth revision is a charm and I only cried three times while writing it.

Self-doubt is a motivation killer. One of my biggest struggles was accepting that I'm not perfect. I don't mean that I stood in front of the mirror every morning chanting, "Mirror, mirror on the wall, who's the fairest one of all?" I mean that I constantly second-guessed every paper that I wrote because I didn't think that it was exactly how it needed to be. In grad school, you bring your own unique perspective and expertise to the table. It's okay to argue and criticize. Newsflash: your professors are a wealth of knowledge, but they don't know everything, and the best ones know and embrace this. They are interested in hearing what you have to say and what you've experienced. Just be prepared to back it up. It is possible to be creative and unique while still being academically credible. Even in the looser confines of writing this chapter I've repeatedly questioned whether or not I'm relaying the perfect message to you. Nothing is perfect. Trying to achieve perfection will only lead to excessive stress, sleepless nights, and possibly excessive drinking. If you're at the point that you're reading this, you have something to offer the world. It's time to look in that mirror and utter the words of the fabulously fictitious Stuart Smalley, Al Franken's character on *Saturday Night Live*, "I'm good enough, I'm smart enough and doggone it, people like me!"

I am not going to go into an in-depth explanation of what causes self-doubt, nor will I give you a 10-step plan to overcome it. My best piece of advice is to talk to your peers. Come to understand that you are not alone in your despair. I once had a great conversation with "that one guy" who always had the exemplary paper, who was the golden child of the program, and who graduated at the top of the class. He was miserable. He confided to me that every waking moment that he wasn't at work he was suffocating in the quest to achieve perfection. He told me how much it bothered him that people thought that everything came so easy for him when he was basically falling apart from anxiety and exhaustion. Now on that encouraging note, I'll share a few things that helped me gain back my self-confidence.

Come up with a manageable game plan, but also know that life happens and your game plan will fall apart at times. One of my biggest problems was that I had a tendency to focus on the overall picture. My problem was that the overall picture came at me like King Kong and I was Jessica Lange (or Fay Wray or Naomi Watts, depending on your generation) tied up on the sacrificial altar waiting to be eaten alive. Break everything into manageable short-term goals and celebrate the small victories. Take a few moments after each accomplishment to celebrate being one step closer to where you need to be. Don't let your passion be eaten alive by the perceived big scary beast in front of you. After all, Kong really did love Anne and she grew to love him for all that he was. Don't let beauty's insecurities kill the beast.

GET INVOLVED

Another way to build your motivation is to put yourself in situations that force you to feel good about yourself. My friends eventually quit inviting me places because whenever they would ask me to do something I would always be busy volunteering somewhere, attending a workshop, or serving on some sort of committee. Someone once gave me the advice, "Don't get overinvolved, it looks bad on your resume, like you're trying too hard." Okay, well, challenge accepted. Personally, I've never thrown myself into something for the sole purpose of making myself look good, that's just an added bonus. I involve myself for the experience and knowledge that I gain, for the people and the feeling of accomplishment. You will be writing papers in grad school. You will be doing research in grad school. If you are immersed in situations in which you are constantly learning and experiencing, this process is going to be not just less overwhelming but it's going to be more natural and real.

Getting involved can be a bit scary, especially if you're a shy introverted creature such as myself, but it opens up a whole new world of knowledge and professional ties. Create opportunities for yourself. Don't wait for them to come to you. If there are volunteer opportunities that directly relate to your area of study, take them. If you can attend conferences or seminars to expand your knowledge and connections, go to them. Not only will it help you be more confident in your classes, but it will also help you out as you transition into your new career. I live in a fairly large city, and inevitably wherever I go, I run into either someone I know or who knows someone that I know through connections that I've made. It's quite the confidence booster when you introduce yourself to someone and their first response is, "Oh hey, I've heard of you, it's a pleasure to meet you." Mission accomplished.

> Status Update: Dropped my oldest son off at college today. I'm not sure if my heart palpitations are from the fact that I am old enough to have a kid in college or if it's because I'm having flashbacks of everything I ever did when I left home to become a responsible adult.

FINDING YOUR ERIK

I had a few crossover classes within my program in which there was a mixture of grad and undergrad students. If I were a hugger, there would have been several times where I would have gone up and put my arms around them just to help relieve a little of the deer-in-the-headlight looks that were plastered on their faces. On the other hand, there were the students that were clearly annoyed because this class was seriously cutting into their prep time before the next frat party. I get it. I had a fabulous time as an undergrad, maybe a little too fabulous. As a small-town girl, who spent a huge part of her academic years sporting one of those plaid Catholic schoolgirl uniforms that many a fantasy is made of, I was ready to break free, leave the chicken coop behind me, and experience whatever life had to offer. But now we're adults. We've lived and learned. The knowledge gained from experiencing life is invaluable. I was miserable in my career choice for a long time but didn't have the motivation to make a change because there was nothing that I really had a burning passion for. And then I found my "Erik."

Erik is a little boy on the autism spectrum that I worked with after I walked away from my previous career, and by walked away I mean got laid off and never looked back. His story is one of challenges, injustices, and victories. It was because of him that I decided to go to graduate school and make a career change. Because of him I strive every day to learn more, to challenge myself and others and to succeed, and to fight for what I believe in. It's because of him that I am sitting here today, encouraging you to sweep all obstacles aside and become the person that you were born to be. Your Erik doesn't necessarily have to be a person, it doesn't need to be a specific situation, it just needs to be something that drives you to lose that self-doubt, knock out the negative thoughts, and climb to the top of that metaphorical mountain. Your Erik will push you through the highs and the lows and encourage you to take the bull by the horns and shout "Party On!"

CONCLUSION

Status Update: Well, I missed my graduation ceremony today because my son was competing at State. Fortunately for me, I was just accepted into my next degree program, so I'll get another chance in a couple of years. What the hell am I thinking?

Not only did I survive graduate school, but I'm going back for more. Will I take my own advice? Make the most of relationships (and even become more of a social animal), rid that self-doubt monkey from my back, throw myself into what is happening around me (and make my own happenings)? Perhaps, but I'll be cursing myself with every word. I will also be crossing things out and making notes in the margins, and that's okay—nobody's perfect. The thing that won't change is my constant need to evolve as a person, the motivation to find inspiration in every corner of my life and the desire to follow my passion. So, now it's time for me to kick you out of my bed. If hooker boots suit you, throw them on. If Poe is a little too dark for you, recite some Hemingway, Dickinson, or even Dr. Seuss, in your head, whatever works. Find your Erik, follow your passions, and have a hell of a good time while doing it.

"True, nervous, very, very dreadfully nervous I had been and am…" There's nothing wrong with being a little mad.

CHAPTER SIXTEEN

Seeing the Stars

REBECCA ZIMMER

"When it is dark enough, you can see the stars," Charles A. Beard (quoted in Secord, 1941).

INTRODUCTION

Throughout the course of obtaining a graduate degree, life, unfortunately, does not stop. If it did, then major life crises could be faced at a later—and, one supposes, better—time. There are any number of life events that can add stress to a graduate program, including illness or death of a loved one, personal illness, divorce (his or her own or that of a parent or other close family member), the necessity of spending time apart from a spouse or significant other, among many other events with long-term consequences. These issues often occur at the most inconvenient time during the graduate program, and, if not dealt with, can lead to both mental and physical ramifications. While everyone deals with stress differently, an unanticipated crisis can leave the student feeling alone in experiencing these types of stresses.

Despite the fact that a student might feel alone in their experience with the negative, they are not— others have been through situations that, while they may not be identical, are similar in the levels of stress they trigger. There is no way to compare the stresses brought on by different people's situations, and no one situation is necessarily worse than another. Although it can be tempting to compare people's bad situations, this practice lends itself to feeling that one's stress must be less than someone else's since some situations may seem like they are less horrible than another.

In some cases there will be people who indicate that a student should just deal with the stress. There may be those who even state that because one person faced a particular disaster and was able to get through it easily that everyone should be able to manage their stress as easily. However, each person has the right to cope with stress in the way that he or she sees best fits the situation—whether others understand the ways in which a person is coping or not. Indeed, people must cope with their crises in an intensely personal way; if they do not, they are liable to have more problems dealing with their feelings later. Any number and type of situation can act as a long-term, significant stressor.

TYPES OF STRESSORS

All kinds of life events can cause stress—good as well as bad. Good life events, such as getting engaged or married, and becoming a parent, are all significantly stressful. However, the happiness that accompanies these events often mitigates some of the negative effects of the stress they inflict. Bad life events, on the other hand, can inflict long-term stresses that have no mitigating factors. No two people have exactly the same types of events happen to them, and they certainly do not react the same way to the stress involved. In some cases the blows seem to just keep coming, one right after the other, which can increase the stress. The following circumstances actually happened to people I know, though I have changed names in order to protect their privacy.

Ally went to the school clinic in her third year to get a prescription for hormonal birth control. When her test results came back, the doctor asked her to come back to the clinic to get them. After waiting—alone—for 2 hours, Ally was told that she was as close to cervical cancer as she could be and not have cancer. She had to have two surgeries to remove the abnormal cells.

Joshua got married the October before he began his doctoral program. His wife was unable to find a position in the same area as his school. This resulted in his moving hours away from her, while he began his graduate program. After a few weeks in school, he began to develop sleeping issues. Between his lack of sleep and the stress of being away from his wife, Joshua began to have panic attacks. Sometimes these episodes would occur in the middle of the night, making them more difficult for him to deal with.

While studying for his Comprehensive Exams, Bryce was also trying to deal with the serious illness of his father. Additionally, he was newly diagnosed with

ADHD. While this was difficult enough, he is a first-generation student, and thus, his family did not understand why he was unable to drive several hours home to spend time with his uncommunicative father while his mother took spontaneous trips. He was unable to work while he sat with his father, because the television was on (at high volume) at all times. Bryce's father recently passed away, but the stress has only changed, not been relieved, because he is suffering from some feelings of (undeserved) guilt. These feelings made studying even more difficult, and postponed his exams.

From the beginning of her graduate career, Mackenzie has been her mother's caregiver. Her mother suffers from both a mental and a physical disorder. Due to these conditions, Mackenzie must closely monitor her mother's food and medicine. She has to have her mother keep a food and medicine diary, checking the entries several times a week. Additionally, she must accompany her mother to all of her doctor's appointments, creating frequent scheduling conflicts.

Jack had issues even before he arrived at his graduate program. Very soon after he began his move, his car broke down. This required the rental of a car, spending money to have his fixed, and driving back home after the car had been fixed to pick it up. Obviously, this cost money, something most graduate students are short on anyway, and put him behind in his assignments. Additionally, he discovered that the people from whom he was renting his apartment were renters themselves, meaning that they were renting to him illegally, and he could be evicted if the homeowners found out. This meant he had to move 2 months after starting the program. Additionally, he moved a day's drive from his fiancée, causing further stress, all on top of beginning a graduate program.

My Oma (grandma) became ill and moved in with my parents shortly after I began my doctoral program. I was able to see her at Christmas that year, but by that time she had been put under hospice (end-of-life) care, and I knew it was unlikely that I would ever see her again. I was right. She died in April of my second semester. Additionally, I was unable to go to the memorial service, because I was teaching when they held it during summer term.

That same year, in early December, my dad was hospitalized. The doctors told us that he would be fine, but I went home early anyway. He was released the day after I returned; however, after a bad night at home and feeling bad all morning the next day, we called an ambulance to take him back to the hospital. By that evening, he was in the intensive care unit, on a respirator. Within the week we were told that there was no chance for him to live off the machines, and that he likely did not have very long left even with medical support, and were given the choice to remove life support. After we made the decision (the right decision) to remove life support, he breathed on his own for about 30 minutes and then passed away—10 days before Christmas. We held the service a week later.

While all of this was going on my Poppop's (grandfather) mental and physical condition were deteriorating quickly. He was too ill to come to my dad's funeral or to my brother's wedding the following June. His condition continued to deteriorate over the next year and a half, and he passed away a year and a half later. Between these losses, I was also trying to deal with my grandma's cancer diagnosis, classes, and studying for Comprehensive exams, which were obviously stressful in and of themselves.

My point is that there is no one terrible thing that could happen. The stressful events that happen in your life are stressful because they happened to you. It would be unreasonable to ask someone else to be stressed due to my life crises, and I certainly cannot understand how stressed someone else feels due to their life. Life happens and it can be extremely stressful—but there are ways to deal with the stresses. I have detailed a few below, but you should definitely look for what works best for you.

DISCLOSURE

Perhaps the most important thing that a student can do is to talk to his or her professors about what is happening. This is particularly crucial if a death or divorce happens in the middle of the semester. Professors can, and often will, rearrange due dates, allow for missed classes, or offer an incomplete for the course. They cannot make any accommodations if they are unaware of the problem, though. Even if the event does not happen during the semester, it can be good to inform professors of what happened, so they are aware that there may be days or classes during which you are more affected than others. Not all professors will be willing to make modifications, and some may tell you that you just need to deal with the issues, but informing them is an important step in the process. Even if one professor is unwilling to work with you, others may offer some type of adjustment, which will help when dealing with classes in which the professor was not willing to change anything for you.

MAINTAIN PHYSICAL HEALTH

Maintaining (or improving) your health can be a useful way to alleviate stress. When a stressful event occurs, it often becomes difficult to think or work as fast as one was previously able. I often found it difficult to concentrate when attempting to read or write for class, which made it a longer process than it normally would have been. When work for school begins taking more time, it is tempting to not take the time to do other things. Thus, it becomes tempting to rely on take-away or delivery meals because they are quick and easy. However, particularly if you were in the habit of eating well prior to the event, this type of shortcut can often make you feel ill. Feeling unwell then adds to your stress level, feeding the problem you already had, and making it worse.

Making healthy meals at home can help in two ways. First of all, the creative outlet of cooking can provide stress release and a rest for your brain. This time away from both schoolwork and thoughts of the stressor acts as a mental break and can leave you much more able to concentrate on your work. Secondly, and more importantly, people who cook at home generally do eat more healthfully, and your physical health is tied directly into your stress levels.

People often find it difficult to make the time to work out when they are dealing with huge amounts of stress. It can be easy to push this to the back burner when it is something you do not particularly enjoy anyway (guilty!). However, even if you do not enjoy working out, and it is a struggle to make yourself do it, the health benefits can help you to get through the stress. Indeed, exercise can clear your mind and give you time to think, while the endorphins produced can help to raise your general mood.

Just taking a walk in the fresh air can help. While walking outside is not always possible, due to weather conditions in the area, even walking on a treadmill can bring a new perspective and clarity. Most people probably do not have a tread-mill (or other exercise equipment) in their home, but as a general rule, as a student you should have access to your school's fitness facilities, which will have a range of machines. Additionally, they may also offer fitness classes as well as personal train-ing, or swimming facilities, if that is your preference. It is just a matter of looking into what your school might offer you in this regard.

Both working out and eating well will help to mitigate the internal stresses of graduate school and the external stresses of bad situations. Maintaining (or improving) your physical health generally helps you to feel better. Feeling better, even if it is only in a physical sense, lessens mental stress.

CULTIVATE SPIRITUAL HEALTH

Another alleviating factor can be found in personal belief systems. If you have a belief in a higher power, then this can bring great comfort. Prayer can bring peace that would not otherwise be easy to come by. Additionally, attending a church, temple, mosque, or synagogue (or some other place of worship) can help you to put your life in perspective. People who believe in a higher order or power sometimes fall away at times of crisis, and if they are graduate students, who are incredibly busy anyway, it is that much easier to neglect the spiritual portion of their lives. If this is not something that brings solace, then it is not a good strategy; however, if it is comforting, it is important to keep up with it.

Even if you do not believe in a higher power, taking the time to meditate can help with stress levels. Simply sitting quietly and attempting to clear your mind is also a good way to get in touch with how you are feeling about not only the external stressor but also your feelings about graduate school and your workload. Sitting calmly and collecting your thoughts can also help you to take stock of your overall mental health and well-being, which can suffer because of school and external stress.

CARE FOR YOUR MENTAL HEALTH

As with your health and your spiritual life, it can be easy to find yourself neglecting your friendships. Sometimes it is not even that you feel too busy to go out or just hang out; instead, it is an overwhelming apathy toward the activity proposed. It can even be that when you made the plans you wanted to participate, yet when the time comes to get ready to go out, it just does not seem worth the effort. It is though. When you withdraw from friends, you are left with less in the way of a support system for the stresses you are under. Also, it leaves you with no one to whom you can vent your frustrations when they are overwhelming. Furthermore, having people around who are upbeat and positive can help to alleviate some of the stress. It is especially important to have friends who are positive, in that they do not drag your mood downward when it is already likely that you will have tendencies in that direction. Additionally, it's easy when you are under significant stress to have a negative attitude toward other people, and having friends who are positive can help mitigate that tendency.

Friends can be very helpful to talk to; however, depending on the levels of stress you are feeling, and how well you are coping with them, you may find it helpful to find a professional to talk to. Many colleges and universities have counseling resources that graduate students are able to use either free or at a significantly reduced cost. If your school does not provide these services, they may offer an insurance plan that could cover some of the costs of sessions.

Talking through the events that caused the stress or just talking with someone about how demanding graduate school is can be a good way to cope. Additionally, professional counselors or psychologists can offer strategies to deal with new challenges so that you are better able to deal with issues as they arise. In some cases, they may feel that you need to talk to a medical doctor about a prescription anti-anxiety or anti-depressant. Again, most schools have a clinic or some sort of health services that grad students may use at little or no cost, so that students who feel the need can talk to someone about the possibility of a prescription.

CONCLUSION

One of the best things you can do when trying to deal with these types of stressors is to take time out for yourself. Do something that you enjoyed before the stress event happened. Taking your mind off the work you have to do and clearing your head a little bit can help you be more successful when trying to concentrate on school. Additionally, if the activity is something you have to concentrate on (i.e., cooking, playing a complicated video game, making a craft project, etc.) then it acts as a distraction to the stresses of life.

When it comes down to it, though, it is possible that none of these things will help deal with both the stresses of school and the external stresses of life. If the time comes that you are unable to deal with both, then the best option may be to take a semester off school. Many programs offer the option to take a semester's leave of absence, without repercussion. In some instances, it may be that you would forfeit your assistantship (if you have one); however, it is extremely important to take care of yourself. Staying in school at the expense of your mental or physical health is not going to help anyone, and it will hurt you. You need to pay attention to the way that you feel, or you may have an unfortunate outcome—staying in class when you are unable to concentrate just wastes your time and money—because you did not necessarily learn the things you needed to, and your grades may suffer.

Unfortunately, when graduate school begins, life does not end. There are many external factors that can cause extensive stress that must be dealt with during the process of gaining a graduate degree. There are strategies to deal with these issues, and I have tried to indicate a few here. However, the best way to deal with stress for one person may not work as well for another person. Try several ways to deal with the stress, knowing that you are not alone, and that many other graduate students have also dealt with personal disasters or issues that sparked long-term stress during their time in graduate school. Always remember, even when you feel alone, you are not.

REFERENCE

Secord, A. H. (1941). Condensed history lesson. *Reader's Digest, 38* (226).

CHAPTER SEVENTEEN

You Can Actually Enjoy Your Life While in Graduate School. How? Don't Procrastinate

ALISON S. MARZOCCHI

INTRODUCTION

I feel like a unicorn. I am a successful graduate student who is generally stress-free and who genuinely enjoys my life. Believe it or not, we may be hard to find, but graduate students like this exist. If you happen to find another unicorn, I guarantee we have something in common: we don't procrastinate.

There is one single tip that will enable you to have a positive experience in graduate school: don't procrastinate. This advice is not new; several authors have documented the prevalence and impact of procrastination in academic settings (Bhavsar, 2005; Rabin, Fogel, & Nutter-Upham, 2011; Roberts, 2010; Sheppard, Nayyar, & Summer, 2000). Although I did not consult these works in the writing of this chapter and speak only from my own experience, interested readers are encouraged to source these references to gain a deeper understanding. It almost feels silly to write a chapter about banning procrastination as it is so glaringly obvious to me that this would be so simple to implement, yet I am always shocked to discover how many graduate students choose to procrastinate in their studies. If you are a student who chooses to procrastinate, I am hoping this chapter will encourage you to break this habit and support you in doing so.

The thing that is the most nonsensical to me regarding procrastination is that you know you have things to do and you know that you're eventually going to be able to find the time to do them, so why wait to find that time? Why not just find that time now, rather than stressing yourself into a frenzy at the last minute? Why not get things done early so that you can spend the remaining free time doing things that are enjoyable? Easy questions, I know!

To me, lingering assignments are much like dirty dishes in the sink. Of course you don't want to do those dishes now. Nobody likes doing dishes. But, is there ever going to be a better time to do them than now? Of course not. It's only going to get worse. The dishes are just going to sit and fester and you're going to feel annoyed by them every time you glance at the sink. Similar to your lingering assignments, you know you're going to end up doing the dishes eventually. Eventually, you will somehow muster up the motivation and find the time. If you can find the time later, you can find the time now. Just do the dishes now. I would bet that if someone conducted a study where they investigated the dishwashing habits of people who procrastinate with their graduate studies versus people who don't, you would find clean sinks in the homes of the non-procrastinators. Would you be at all surprised to know that my dishes are clean right now? Or that there are never dishes left lingering in my sink? Well, there aren't, ever, because I have banned procrastination from my everyday living.

DON'T MAKE EXCUSES

If you're procrastinating, you'll be able to come up with 100 excuses about why you can't transcribe that data or write that paper or even respond to that e-mail...but the thing is, you know you're going to have no choice but to find the time to do it eventually. Guess what? I "don't have time" to write this chapter right now. As I type this, I have lesson plans to write, a stack of textbooks that need to be coded for my second line of research, a literature review that I need to expand for my assistantship, a conference talk that I need to practice, a manuscript that needs to be prepared for journal submission, a brand new condo that needs to be painted, a friend who needs to vent about her new job, a dinner that's not about to cook itself, and so forth. The list doesn't end. It never will.

Further, I'm writing this chapter several weeks before it's due. Why? Because guess what's going to happen over the next few weeks. If you guessed that magically my schedule would open up wide and I would suddenly have the perfect time slot in which to write this chapter, stress-free and completely mentally prepared to do so, you'd be dead wrong. So stop telling yourself that's going to happen. All that's going to happen over the next few weeks is that I'm going to have even more items added to that list. The list never stops, it's never empty, you never finish it. From now until the end of graduate school, and likely for the rest of your life, you're going to have things to do, so I implore you to do them now, not later.

BENEFITS OF BANNING PROCRASTINATION

There are many benefits to banning procrastination. In this subsection, I will share some of the benefits that I have experienced. My intention is not to brag or sound superior to my peers. In fact, I am nowhere near the smartest person among my peers, nor am I the most experienced or the most educated. There is one thing, however, that I can confidently claim. I am the best at simply getting stuff done. There have been many benefits to this. For instance, among the cohort of 18 students with whom I started my doctoral program, I was the first to defend my dissertation and I was also the first to get a job. These are two generally unrelated events but I do not believe that they are a coincidence; again, they are a direct result of my conscious decision to ban procrastination. Another benefit was that I was able to find the time to further myself academically in many other ways outside of my graduate program (and you can experience this too!). This included tutoring local low-income high school students, advising an undergraduate club, taking on several extra writing assignments that led to publications, regularly seeing guest speakers on campus (and I'm talking about ones that aren't required by my program), and sitting in on unrequired courses simply because they interested me.

Perhaps counterintuitively, I was not only the first in my cohort to defend my dissertation and get a job, and one of the few to do the above-and-beyond work listed above, but I also had the most active social life. Your graduate experience does not need to be one of misery and isolation. If you choose to ban procrastination, you too can find enjoyment in your graduate study years. While many of my peers would be scrambling at the last minute to get work done, I was finding plenty of open time slots in my schedule to fill with activities I enjoyed. There were very few ways in which my life resembled the lives of my graduate school peers. I spent small chunks of time doing a number of different things while my peers generally spent all of their time doing only one thing: their graduate studies.[1] During the time in my graduate program, I went to dozens of concerts, vacationed, went to the beach, went to parties, played volleyball, played softball, did yoga several times a week, read (and not just for research, but for pleasure!), made it home to see my family once a month, etc. Unlike most, my social life did not slow down substantially when I started graduate school. How is it that I had the exact same amount of work as my peers yet they found little time to do anything else? How is it that I was held to the exact same expectations as they were yet they were feeling so much more stress? How is it that they were "spending so much more time" (more on this later) on their graduate studies, yet accomplishing less? By now, I think you know the answer to these questions.

PROCRASTINATION-BANNING TECHNIQUES

The first step is to simply stop procrastinating. To do so, you must recognize and take responsibility for your previous procrastinating behaviours. You must be hard on yourself. Every time you don't work on an assignment that you intend to work on, you make a conscious decision to not work on it. If you procrastinate, you are actively choosing to procrastinate. It's that simple. To think of it any other way is useless and unproductive. The only way a task is going to get done is if you do it. Although I believe that banning procrastination is as simple as making a decision to stop procrastinating, the subsections that follow will offer more concrete guidelines for how you can achieve this.

Make a List

No matter how many things you have to do, you can realistically only work on one thing at a time. I highly recommend maintaining a current and dynamic list of everything you need to do. I have one master list of all of the big tasks that need to be done and then I keep track of daily to-do lists. Sometimes I schedule something to do on a particular day months in advance. As soon as a new major task comes up, I add it to the master list and then I go to my calendar and schedule timeslots to work on the various pieces of that task.

Every night before I go to bed, I look at my to-do list for the next day and I reorganize it so that it is listed in the order in which I will do each item. In doing this, I wrap my mind around what I need to accomplish the next day, and I wake up ready to tackle the first item. A seemingly daunting number of assignments is suddenly transformed into a manageable sequence of tasks.

Keeping a to-do list helps me to avoid procrastination in several ways. For one, I rarely spend time spinning my wheels stressing about everything I need to do and trying to figure out what to do first. There is no need for me to make decisions on what to do at any given moment because the list has already decided. I surrender my power to the list. The list tells me what to do, and so I do it.

In addition, when maintaining a current and dynamic to-do list, I don't have the option to procrastinate. I have already planned my tasks for each day far in advance, and I know there is little room for things to be rescheduled. If I don't finish the task today, I know how difficult it will be to find an available timeslot on a different day. The task must be done today, and so I do it today.

The list also helps me to keep things in perspective. The list never ends, and it never will, but all you have the power to do is check off one item at a time. Allowing the list to run your life alleviates some of the stress of graduate school. It reminds you that you are but one person capable of working on one thing at a time. The list simply tells you what that one thing is at any given moment.

Finishing this chapter is the last item that needs to be checked off my list today. I'm about to check it off. Tomorrow is a new day with a new list. By this time tomorrow, those items will be checked off that list. I won't make excuses, I won't dillydally. I'll get right to the list as soon as I get up and I will do what it tells me to do. It's honestly as simple as that. Keep track of the things you need to do and...just do them.

Prioritize

When you first start graduate school, every single thing that you're assigned will feel like it is of equal importance to everything else. This, particularly if you've gone straight through your schooling, will likely be the first time in your life that you feel like you don't actually have the time you need to do all of the things that you need to do. For this reason, when you first start graduate school you will find yourself spending 20 hours on an assignment that is only worthy of 2 hours of your time. This may cause you to rush on a different assignment that is of greater value. It is crucial that you start actively keying into which assignments are more or less important.

I cannot directly advise you on which of your tasks will be more or less important because this is quite discipline- and degree-specific, but in general, tasks that further your own research (think...which items will eventually have an impact on your curriculum vitae) are of higher value than a run-of-the-mill class assignment. Of course, even if your curriculum vitae is carved in gold, you can't get a job if you fail your classes. Thus, I am not saying that you shouldn't do your course assignments, but can you produce a product that is worthy enough in 2 hours' time rather than spending 20 hours on it? As time goes by in your graduate studies, you will recognize that your precious time is better spent on some tasks than others.

How does prioritizing help you to ban procrastination? For one, when you get better at prioritizing, you will get better at constructing those invaluable to-do lists that I spoke of in the previous section. You will learn how to weigh the priority of an item into the construction of your to-do lists so that you will be maximally efficient each day. Additionally, identifying whether a task is of high or low priority will help you in the (rare) instance when you actually cannot finish your to-do list. What task can be rescheduled for a different day and/or rescheduled for a much shorter timeslot than you had originally planned? By effectively prioritizing, you will become better at giving yourself less opportunity to procrastinate on the tasks that are of the greatest importance.

Set a Time Limit

Setting a time limit is a procrastination-banning technique directly related to prioritizing. Remember that hypothetical low-priority assignment that you spent 20 hours on when you could have completed it in 2? Don't give yourself a 20-hour timeslot to work on it. I have found that how long an assignment takes you to complete is generally equal to the amount of time that you give yourself to complete it. If you block off 20 hours to work on the task, you will spend 20 hours on it. If you give yourself 2, you will somehow find a way to finish it in 2.

Of course, I must be realistic and recognize that this cannot always be the case. Similar to prioritizing, you'll get better at setting time limits as you progress through graduate school. When you first start, you will likely have no idea how long it takes you to read a 30-page article or create a conference presentation. Setting time limits will take practice at first and will involve much trial and error, but in time you'll learn your own pace. This will help you to create ever-more-productive and maximally efficient to-do lists!

Further, when you set a specific time limit for a task, you will maximize your efficiency in working on this task. If you block off the entire day to do something that should only take a few hours, I doubt you'll actually spend the entire day actively engaged in working on the assignment. More likely, you'll spend much of the day wasting time, doing other things that pop into your head that "need" to be done at that moment, or thinking about doing the assignment rather than actually doing it. Setting a tight time limit forces you to avoid procrastination and ensures that you must get right on task. Rather than leaving the day wide open to work on things, I recommend planning specific and manageable tasks to do that day (I'm referencing your mighty to-do list!). Most of my graduate school peers do not do this. They will block off an entire weekend to do an assignment that I know I can finish in 5 hours. I'll finish it in 5 hours, usually on Friday afternoon or Saturday morning, and then I'll spend the rest of the weekend having fun. They'll spend 30 hours "working" on that exact same assignment. In the end, they've probably only done 5 hours of quality work (maybe less!), but somehow they've managed to stretch those 5 hours of work into a 30-hour timeslot. They rarely find the time to have fun on the weekends.

Treat Deadlines as Deadlines

Shockingly, I discovered that many of my professors were allowing my peers to turn in assignments late. As you would imagine, I do not condone this. My opinion aside, even if your professors will allow you to turn in assignments late, you should never take them up on this. To start, it will only allow you to develop (or reinforce) bad habits, such as procrastination, that you will need to learn to break later. Why not break those habits now? After all, you will likely not have the "luxury" of turning in assignments late in your career. If you are choosing to remain in academia, you will have conference proposals with strict deadlines and lesson plans that must be completed before the unwavering start time of class. Shouldn't graduate school serve to adequately train you for the next phase of your life? Now is the time to start treating your deadlines as deadlines.

Additionally, if you do not complete your assignments on time and you allow them to linger into winter "break" or summer "break," you are taking precious time away from working on other endeavours. These "breaks" are the perfect opportunity for you to further your own research or take on extra projects. By procrastinating and missing deadlines during the semester, you will always be behind and it will be nearly impossible to ever dig yourself out of it.

Bribe Yourself

Although most of my motivation to ban procrastination is intrinsic, I am in no way opposed to extrinsic motivators. On days when my own internal motivation isn't strong enough, I will shamelessly bribe myself with extrinsic rewards.

Sometimes, embarrassingly, my extrinsic motivators are not too far from a dog's treat. I'm not too ashamed to admit that I've rewarded myself on several occasions with five Reese's Pieces for each page I read from a handbook chapter. Hey, whatever works. More typically, I will give myself until midnight to complete my to-do list. If I finish my list before midnight, I will allow myself to choose anything I want to watch on Netflix. If midnight rolls around and I'm not finished, I keep working and I must go to bed immediately when I'm done. I didn't earn my Netflix. There were many nights where 10:00 p.m. rolled around and I stepped on my productivity accelerator because I realized I wasn't working at the right pace for my midnight deadline. I hated the thought of going straight to bed rather than giving myself 22 minutes to turn off my brain and melt on the couch while watching an episode of *The Office* (and maybe popping a few Reese's Pieces). I've avoided procrastination and completed many assignments because of this silly extrinsic motivator. You simply need to find something that works for you.

Many of my graduate school peers have asked me how I'm able to get everything done so far in advance. I've often shared this tip with them, and they've all responded in the same way—that they've "tried" doing this before but they end up eating the Reese's or watching the show anyway. Did you just see me roll my eyes? Obviously these bribes only work if you actually do them, just like your work only gets done if you actually do it.

Do More

This may seem counterintuitive, but if you find yourself procrastinating in your studies, you should consider loading up your schedule with more things to do. The more you need to do, the easier it will be to get things done. If you have more time available to allow things to linger, you will be much more likely to let things linger. If you have one available timeslot to do a task, you will have no choice but to do that task in that timeslot.

Are you concerned about overexerting yourself? I find that, in general, I always have time to do whatever I set out to do. I believe that there's no such thing as too little time, there's only too much procrastination. I complete an "impossible" amount of tasks on a near-daily basis and I still have plenty of time to have fun.

On two separate occasions, a faculty member approached several students in my program with an opportunity to co-author a paper. On the first occasion, I was the only student to accept the offer. On the second occasion, seven students originally accepted but only three persevered to the completion of the paper. Both papers resulted in a publication on my curriculum vitae. In the end, each of these assignments took only a few hours of extra work. There was no question that I was going to be able to find a few extra hours to take advantage of these opportunities, which may have ultimately contributed to me obtaining my dream job. The thing is, you have these hours available, you just need to actively find and use them. The only way things get done is if you do them (is there an echo in the room?).

Schedule Your Social Life

Last, I recommend that you actively schedule your social life. Just as you schedule your daily to-do lists around your major tasks, you can schedule your school work around social events. If I find out about a concert I want to go to, I buy the concert tickets. If one of my friends is having a party back home, I RSVP for the party. So long as I know of these events far enough in advance, I know I can work my to-do lists around them. If anything, scheduling my social life forces me to be more productive in my studies; it has a positive impact on many of the abovementioned tips. Just as your school work won't get done if you don't do it, your social life won't happen if you don't choose to be social. It also won't happen if you procrastinate your life away.

CONCLUSION

Throughout this chapter, I sought to share the many benefits of avoiding procrastination in the hopes of enticing you to join me in banning it from your graduate studies. I have highlighted that procrastination is a deliberate choice that you make, and a choice that you have complete control over. However, in the interest of being perfectly candid I must warn you that once you learn to completely banish procrastination from your graduate studies you will inevitably face one major challenge: finding other unicorns with whom to spend all of your new-found free time!

NOTE

1. Although I argue that most of the time they're not actually doing their work, but procrastinating doing it.

REFERENCES

Bhavsar, V. M. (2005). How to survive, thrive, and learn science in graduate school: One student's perspective. *Journal of Natural Resources and Life Sciences Education, 34*, 36–39.

Rabin, L. A., Fogel, J., & Nutter-Upham, K. E. (2011). Academic procrastination in college students: The role of self-reported executive function. *Journal of Clinical and Experimental Neuropsychology, 33*(3), 344–357. doi:10.1080/13803395.2010.518597

Roberts, C. M. (2010). *The dissertation journey: A practical and comprehensive guide to planning, writing, and defending your dissertation.* Thousand Oaks, CA: Corwin.

Sheppard, J. P., Nayyar, P. R., & Summer, C. E. (2000). Managing your doctoral program: A practical orientation. *Production and Operations Management, 9*(4), 414–437. doi:10.1111/j.1937–5956.2000.tb00467.x

PART FIVE

Studying Overseas:
Student Perspectives

CHAPTER EIGHTEEN

17 Hours Behind

Studying at a Distance

ALISON HICKS

INTRODUCTION

I blame it on the *Flying Doctors*. This 1980s mini-series about rural health professionals who flew around the outback soon grew to characterize the very essence of Australia to me—the hot sun and the lack of vegetation, but above all, the vast open spaces where distance was no object. Along with stories about outback school radio, I suppose it was only natural that when I realised that my PhD would have to be in a distance program, my thoughts automatically turned to Australia. Yet, despite the fact that communication technologies have improved slightly since the days of Dr. Callaghan, I could tell that my family and friends had major doubts about my sanity. How on earth could I complete a graduate degree located 8000 miles and 17 time zones away from my supervisor?

Whether you're interested in studying in Australia or some other far-flung destination, this chapter will be useful to anyone who is thinking of studying abroad from the comfort of their own home. While studying at a distance is becoming more common, and, occasionally, seen as the future of higher education, many people still seem to find the idea quite unusual. Yet, despite some minor irritations, I maintain that my graduate experience has been immeasurably improved by taking this exciting step. Focusing on my personal experiences as a distance education doctoral student who is living and working full time in the United States while studying part time in Australia, this chapter will center on advice that ranges from the practical, such as time zone navigation and ensuring you are not forgotten, to the economic, such as funding and scholarships, and the more prosaic, such as navigating another university culture and coping with local slang.

NUTS AND BOLTS

The first question that people always ask me when they find out that I am studying my PhD at a distance is how does it all work? In brief, I'm enrolled as a part-time, offshore (international), distance, higher degree by research (HDR) student in the School of Information Studies at Charles Sturt University, which is located in Wagga Wagga, New South Wales, Australia. It's quite a mouthful! I have a primary supervisor who I meet every month via Skype to chat about my reading or to get her feedback about my writing, and a secondary supervisor who I meet less frequently. I attend departmental events through Adobe Connect, and access e-books and journals through the university library with my student login. My PhD program itself is structured by the endorsement of my research proposal, which I have to present during my first 2 years of enrolment; data collection; and writing-up, which are bookended by the (written, rather than oral) examination of my dissertation. As an international distance education student, I have a special category of enrolment that means that I don't have to have an Australian visa. Semesters run from March through June and from July through October.

INTERNATIONAL DISTANCE EDUCATION: BENEFITS AND DRAWBACKS

The second question that people ask me is why Australia? There have been both benefits and drawbacks with my choice of distance study and of my location.

One of the major benefits of the distance PhD has been the ability to work with one of the top researchers in my field. Unable to leave Colorado, yet determined that the PhD was something that I wanted to do, my thoughts had initially turned to several respected doctoral programs nearby. However, I knew that the most exciting research in my area was not taking place within the United States, and that it would have been hard to find a local supervisor who was engaged in this field. By remaining open to the distance option, I was able to choose my PhD program based on my intellectual interests and goals rather than pragmatic reasons of location or what fitted in with my schedule.

I'm not going to lie, another major benefit of studying in Australia is the fact that the full-time program tends to last just 3 years. Having worked and published in the field for almost 10 years, the thought of having to go back to school for another decade of coursework was unappealing, to say the least. Furthermore, one of the major reasons that I wanted to start the PhD was because I already had a clear idea of my topic—in fact, it had been niggling me for years. The Australian system, which, like the British system, is solely based on the dissertation, meant that I could start writing from day one of my enrolment. Even though I eventually chose to do a part-time option, I hope to finish within 4 to 5 years, which is still less time than many full-time PhD programs in the United States.

Flexibility was the final reason why studying abroad appealed to me. As a mature student with family commitments, distance education has taken away relocation, travel, and visa stresses, as well as enabling me to explore an academic career move at my own pace. At the same time, the fact that Australia is so well set up for distance education means that I don't feel like I am missing out. When I initially approached my supervisor to see how she would feel about taking on a graduate student from the other side of the world, she didn't blink an eyelid. In fact, opportunities seemed to have been expressly designed to accommodate students like me. Thus, departmental workshops and talks are regularly streamed online. Student groups and the committee to which I was appointed only met virtually; the library offered to ship me books. CSU also provides travel funds to undertake the endorsement presentation, although they make provision for an online examination if this isn't possible. In other words, as a distance student, I don't feel like a second-class citizen—instead, the university has made me feel like a welcomed and a valued part of the department.

Having said that, the lack of a supportive cohort of fellow students is one of the largest downsides of distance education that I have found. While this is due, in part, to the more individual or personalized nature of Australian doctoral studies, and the university has established a number of formal meetings for graduate students to get to know each other, it's not the same as sharing a relaxing beer at the end of the day. Furthermore, even though, as a part-time student, I have been able to maintain my professional support network in Colorado, I sometimes long to chat to people who are going through the same experiences as me. The isolation can occasionally have more practical drawbacks too—I miss out on the informal learning that occurs through casual departmental conversations about, for example, the best type of microphone to use for field research.

While I have generally felt very welcomed in my department, I've found that it helps to make an extra effort to build connections from afar. People do notice if you take the time to log in to departmental events or workshops, and this also helps to ensure that you are not forgotten. I volunteered for a committee, too, to build relationships beyond my supervisors. One of the ideas that has worked out best for me was asking my supervisor to put me in contact with other students. I Skype regularly with one of the other PhD students in my department, and it's been such a relief to be able to ask her all the questions that I didn't want to bother my supervisor with (questions about the web systems, for example). In addition, make friends with the administrative assistants. It's always a smart move, but doubly important when you're starting out within a completely different system of higher education. Not only do they know all the rules and regulations backwards, but they may also be able to point you in the direction of hidden support services or funding sources from groups or institutions that you might never have heard about.

Financial matters can be a drawback too. There are very few scholarships and funding opportunities available for students who are both international and studying at a distance. And, while I am still eligible for a number of grants in the United States, many are limited to individuals who are pursuing higher education in their home country. Studying at a distance obviously means that I am not eligible for casual work as a research or teaching assistant on campus, either. All of these factors contributed to my decision to maintain my current job and to study part-time. The fluctuating exchange rate can be alarming too. While the strong U.S. dollar is in my favor right now, I'm aware that this might change and the final cost of my fees is not guaranteed. The financial burden may also be increased as you learn about and join new professional associations, or if you have to engage in more conference travel. On the plus side, while international fees in Australia are marginally higher than domestic fees, and legislation to raise more revenue from international students is being considered, my part-time program costs about US $7000/year, which is comparable to non-resident tuition within a U.S. doctoral program, and considerably less than what an international student would pay. Furthermore, you can still claim educational tax credit in the United States.

The other drawback that I have found is the fact that for the first 6 months of my PhD it didn't feel real. I was reading and studying and meeting my supervisor on Skype every month, but until I managed to meet her in person at a conference, it felt a little bit as though I was just playing at being a doctoral student. After we met, though, it felt like a blindfold had been removed from my eyes, and that I had started work in earnest. I don't know whether this dose of reality was due to the fact that it was the first time I had met my supervisor since I enrolled, or if it was because our meeting coincided with her first comments on my writing, or whether this would have happened if I had been studying full time. Whatever the reason, that in-person meeting definitely marked a meaningful moment in my PhD for me. For these reasons, and if circumstances allow it, I would recommend either trying to visit the institution in person during your first year, or meeting up with your supervisor at a conference at least once. While I think that it would be possible to complete the entire course of study without meeting your supervisors, this tactic definitely enabled me to get to discuss issues and future ideas in a more informal context and setting, as well as getting to know my supervisor better.

APPLYING AND CHOOSING A SUPERVISOR

The individual nature of the PhD program, coupled with the pressures of distance education, meant that I knew that I would have to find a flexible supervisor whom I could respect and get on well with for the next 5 years. To this end, I attended one of the major conferences in my field during the summer before I applied to graduate school in order to meet and chat with a number of potential supervisors. This turned out to be a really worthwhile process and saved me from making a poor decision. The lack of in-person contact during the PhD means that your connection with your supervisor is of the utmost importance—so if you can travel to meet people, or at least talk on Skype before you enrol, you will be able to make much more informed decisions. You could also ask to talk to current students, and check how many international or distance students have graduated from the program.

After I had selected my institution, the application process was fairly straightforward, although there were several additional hoops that I had to jump through as an international student. The most time-consuming part of this was having to get my degree certificates and documents notarized—and as the originals were still sitting thousands of miles away in my parents' attic, this proved to be more complicated than I expected. Make sure you have those original documents to hand as you apply. A word of warning about the application software too—universities will never win any awards for simple, easy-to-use websites, and I found that Australian systems are, if anything, worse. Be prepared to tear your hair out over really confusing and ugly web pages.

The challenges don't stop after you've been accepted, either. If, like me, you end up attending an Australian university, you may want to keep the urban dictionary or a guide to Aussie slang (http://www.koalanet.com.au/australian-slang.html) open. The first time my supervisor called someone ridgy-didge, I had to subtly multitask while I found out whether this was good or bad. (If you're interested, it means genuine. Who knew?!)

NEGOTIATING TIME DIFFERENCES

Until you get used to it, the time difference can be hard to get your head round. While I still have quite a lot of flexibility about meeting times, it can take a while to work out calendars and schedules. Furthermore, daylight savings time (which obviously happens at different times of the year in each country) means that the time difference fluctuates. This means that you always have to check the date as well as the time when setting up meetings. I use the World Time Buddy app and web page (http://www.worldtimebuddy.com/) to help me work this out. Make sure you enable time zone support in other software programs too—for example, Doodle (http://doodle.com/), which enables you to poll people for meeting times. Another idea that has worked well for me is to establish the range of times that I will make myself available for meetings. In my case, this is 7 a.m. to 10 p.m., a timeframe that makes it easier for me to say no if I'm tempted by that midnight meeting. A different trick that my supervisor and I use is for us to always meet at the same time in one of our countries. This means that it's just one of us who has to work out the time difference each month. Generally, I've found that people and online workshops accommodate time zones, though, and in time, it becomes second nature.

The seasonal difference isn't so problematic, but it's quite visually disconcerting when you are wrapped up in a woolly sweater, and the people you are chatting with are sweating away in a sleeveless top. Like the time difference, though, you get used to it. The different semester dates can also be hard to get your head round initially for people coming from North America. Generally, universities in the Southern Hemisphere go quiet from December to February, so I have tried to adjust my writing and requests for feedback to come before or after those dates. Application dates are also quite different, so double check this carefully. Be careful, too, when you casually refer to the conference that is happening in spring or fall—always try and specify what month you mean rather than the season.

RESEARCH AND FUNDING

Research, for the most part, has been fairly straightforward, thanks to my university library's great collection of online journals and books. While they offered to ship any physical books that I needed through interlibrary loan, I've found it easier to use the library of the local research university near me in the United States. Public patrons can often purchase a card that will allow them to check out books (my local library charges US $70 per year), or, alternatively, you can use a number of research libraries in person for free. Public patron cards rarely give you access to online journals from home, but most U.S. libraries will allow you to logon to their computers and access journals and databases from onsite. Other tricks that may help include using Google Books (http://books.google.com), especially if you have to check a quote; Hathi Trust (http://www.hathitrust.org/), which gives some free access to older digitized books; and Google Scholar (http://scholar.google.com), where you can often find the full text of academic articles. If all else fails, try the #icanhazpdf hashtag on Twitter.

One other thing to bear in mind is the academic vocabulary differences between countries. Thus, research methods in the United States are called research techniques in Australia, and Australian research methods are U.S. research methodologies. Other tips and tricks include using a cookbook stand if you need to quote or make notes from a book; for anyone who plans to transcribe, investing in a foot pedal with your recording device is a really smart idea. For funding, the best site that I have found is Research Professional (https://www.researchprofessional.com), which I have access to through my university. It enables you to set up funding alerts in your research area, as well as specifying funding sources by your country of origin. My university also offers a small amount of funding for research expenses each year to each student, regardless of their status. This can be used for travel, software, or for expenses incurred during research, such as incentives. Also check professional associations who may often have grants, scholarships, or volunteer conference places for graduate students.

CONCLUSION

While I haven't graduated yet, I can honestly say that starting this PhD has been one of the best decisions that I have ever made. My colleagues say that my face lights up when I talk about my research, and that is due, I think, to the fact that I was able to choose the right program and supervisor for me. The frustrations have been minimal, the benefits have been considerable, and the ability to build global connections has been an added bonus that will, hopefully, serve me well in the future. Some people may consider that Australian higher education is markedly inferior to the U.S. system, but having experienced education on both continents, I feel that, in many respects, the Australian program is actually far more rigorous.

Ultimately, the distance education PhD isn't for everyone. If you are fresh out of a master's program, or feel like you need a very structured educational environment, then distance education may be too flexibly nebulous for you. If, on the other hand, you are organized and motivated or have prior experience in the field, the personalized nature of distance education in Australia means that it can be tailored to your exact needs. And, although this chapter has focused on my experiences in Australia, there are a number of other programs in the United Kingdom and New Zealand, to name but two, that might work equally well for you. Advances in communication technologies have greatly expanded options for tertiary education—so if you'd like to inject your PhD experience with a dose of adventure, give international distance education a go!

CHAPTER NINETEEN

Navigating Academic Culture Shock

Advice for International Students

ALISTAIR KWAN

INTRODUCTION

The aim of this chapter is to help guide your journey, from that initial shock of learning in a U.S. context, and even to the teaching of American students. Ultimately, the experience of studying abroad is not one-way. The experience is cross-cultural, and while you will undoubtedly grow from your experience, so too will those you live among. This chapter offers you important advice on navigating the *academic* culture shock that many international students experience. It begins by exploring cultural differences, and offers advice in choosing programs of study before arriving in the U.S. While the notion of "culture shock" has been written about extensively, I will draw on my own experiences and observations to go beyond what university websites and the research literature have to say.

EXPLORING A DIFFERENT ACADEMIC CULTURE

For students coming from a different educational system and scouting the United States from afar, it can be tricky both choosing a graduate program and thriving while in it. It may also not be obvious at the onset of your studies that your graduate student years offer important opportunities to establish practicalities needed for a life in America, should you wish to stay after graduation.

Coming from afar, your undergraduate education probably did not follow the American-style liberal arts curriculum. American undergraduate degrees have long been grounded in a 19-century ideal of producing citizens active in democratic society. The "liberal" in "liberal arts" is the "liberal" of "liberty," and "arts" includes humanities, sciences, and social sciences (Logan & Curry, 2015). Liberal education is still widely championed as a necessary precursor to both professional and graduate studies, so most American graduate students will have gone through some version of it. Because a liberal curriculum often manifests as breadth, U.S. undergraduates will typically combine topics as diverse as classical history, contemporary media studies, and molecular biology.

You may come with quite different expectations about both work standards and the kinds of work that count as "academic," though this is also an issue for Americans because the graduate and undergraduate curricula are so different. Your culture in an ethnic or regional sense may also differentiate you from your classmates. My classmates and I stumbled sometimes over differences between our Englishes, and also between our assumptions about common knowledge. Much is said about ethnicity-linked differences in academic integrity, but if your goal is academic excellence, this is important to master in any case. The differences cut both ways. I found it strange, for example, that my fellow American students thought it usual to work from translations without also checking the original language, and would never utter the source languages even when quoting. While they had often taken language courses as undergraduates, they hadn't all come to think of translation as a source of bias, nor original-language work as a basic expectation. So, while the literature on international students tends to focus on how we struggle, the fact is that our differences do not always put us on the back foot.

Perhaps more conspicuously, your unfamiliarity with local academic culture may leave you puzzled about how your fellow students operate: where and when they study, and how they engage during class.

CHOOSING A PROGRAM FROM AFAR

Obviously, most international students cannot personally visit multiple institutions, which makes it harder to know about both academic and local culture. But there are ways to scout from a distance (that are also useful to American students).

It is important to distinguish between program and university. Universities pour immense effort into their branding, as you can see on their websites, press releases, and recruitment brochures that they send in the mail. Perhaps that branding matters to you—there is a great deal of prestige in graduating from an Ivy League institution, MIT, Chicago, Berkeley, Stanford. Brand loyalty is often superficial, but it is also practical. One employer told me outright that they wanted my Ivy branding and Britannic cultural affectations to strengthen their image, especially when courting donors. In that context, the university's brand marketing doubles as *your* brand marketing. Perhaps that gives good reason to attend one of those famed institutions.

From a more immediate perspective, you could expect that a wealthy university will have more resources to support your studies, especially if you need exceptional library or museum collections (largely ignored in ranking tables) (Jackson, 2015), fieldwork, laboratory apparatus, or travel to access those elsewhere. You can scout all of that online via each institution's scholarship and fellowship listings, its library and museum catalogs, and internal newsletters congratulating funding recipients and describing their projects. Library and museum resources were very high on my priority list, cutting the range of suitable institutions very short—I was happy to travel for special items (the university's internal funding supported that) but wanted substantial core collections close at hand for day-to-day research. Several friends in experimental high-energy physics, on the other hand, were happy with summer visits to FermiLab (the Fermi National Accelerator Laboratory, near Chicago) and CERN (the European particle physics laboratory straddling Switzerland, France, and Italy).

While the university's central services matter, you also need discipline-specific excellence. For that, you need to focus on departments and programs. There are several ways to go about this. Obviously, you can look at the faculty publication lists ("faculty" in the U.S. generally means academic personnel, whereas "staff" usually means professional and administrative personnel). You can also look at past dissertations (search by advisor and committee member in ProQuest's *Dissertations & Theses* database) to see what sorts of projects they handle, and head to Google to see how their students' careers turned out. Doing this scouting yourself is especially important if your career goals are outside academia, because many programs omit non-academia success stories in their on-line lists of recent graduates. You can also look into where program alumni and current students previously graduated, to gauge whether the program or particular advisors are already accustomed to supporting international students.

Everyday life in a department or program, and even across a university, more broadly, can be very hard to evaluate from afar. It can even be well-hidden during in-person visits. A clandestine visit to a university can furnish valuable insight into openness, collegiality, and competiveness; the speed of life; and the extent of intellectual and cultural stimulation. All it takes is an observant wander around campus, scanning notice boards, overhearing conversations, perhaps sitting in on a few classes incognito. As a foreigner, though, you may struggle to make out those details from a distance. Online virtual tours and lecture recordings are carefully contrived, and often concentrate on iconic landmarks and star performers that parents and tourists like to see, not the spaces and activities in which graduate student life plays out. You may be able to find indirect clues, however. Look for the students' personal web pages where institutional control is less strict—are the students at ease with each other and the faculty, or predominantly alone? Do they mention each other and professors by first name or title and surname? How do they describe their work—do they share as colleagues, or hold back as competitors? The underlying question that you should consider is, do the people of that program seem the sort that you will thrive among?

FINDING A CULTURAL FIT

Finding a good cultural match is, I believe, crucial. I was advised very sternly about this by an American visitor who, after only 10 minutes' conversation, announced that there was only one U.S. university that I should bother with. Attend any other, he cautioned, and I would walk out within a year. For me, his advice seems to have been spot-on. I went where he advised, and I thrived. Part of my context was a strong sense of direction and autonomy, nurtured by a long chain of New Zealand and Australian teachers who knew how to work with that, and indeed considered it a mark of a good student. Not all graduate programs are designed with early autonomy in mind—some curricular schemes plan for its development only after covering canonical groundwork, on the assumption that students coming straight from an American undergraduate program (and possibly not you) need both a firm induction to the norms and a safely paced transition to independence.

Misfit between student and institution has very real consequences. Many students leave graduate study without completing (Golde, 1998). Some students waste years achieving nothing before that happens. In my working life, I once advised a graduate student to end several unproductive years by starting again at another institution that more closely fitted his aspirations and needs. He did exactly that, and after transferring, almost immediately began to thrive. It will be harder to do this as an international student. Quitting may annul your visa, and then you will need a new visa to study at the next institution. It is much better to invest early in finding a good match.

Then there is local culture. It is important that adjusting to local culture does not undermine your academic success, and also worth considering the value of an intercultural experience. But don't be misled by the impression that there is a single "American culture": culture varies widely across the United States, so even American students experience culture shock in other parts of their own country! You can read about local customs and foods in many places, even tourist guidebooks. I found vegetarian dining scarce in much of the country, for example, and even fresh produce—much of New England's is stale after its long journey from California.

The hardest cultural advice to find, in my experience, concerned racial dynamics. I did not expect to be affected by it as much as I was, nor did I expect to be classified as "Asian" (an excessively broad category that does considerable damage in U.S. universities). In fact, many in my circle of international friends found that the endemic racism and segregation was far beyond what they had imagined possible in such a developed country. I dodged a full dose: one prospective institution inadvertently hinted at its racial and gender tensions by packing its most prominent brochures full of anti-stereotype representations. Brochure illustrations are carefully chosen to make a point—specifically to communicate a welcome to people who don't fit the stereotypical moulds—so I became concerned that there was a need to do that quite so prominently, and did not apply. Perhaps I over-interpreted, I often thought, but everyone I have since asked about that campus, including people who've studied or worked there, has said that my assessment was unfortunately spot-on. I did not escape the tension, however. I experienced the no-speak-English assumption, long stares (people actually stopped in their tracks to watch me walk past), and racist jeering. African friends were often grouped in with African American stereotypes, which, given how often classroom dynamics and police brutality feature in both educational research and the national news, provides cause for concern.

My white friends and wife were not exempt either. In large swathes of the city, white people were viewed with suspicion. One friend, out for a relaxing walk, was warned in all seriousness to leave before he got shot. I had an advantage, as in some of those neighborhoods I was perceived as belonging to a "neutral" race. Adults would stop to tell me about the best deals at the supermarket and what clothes I would need for winter. Children would cluster around for high-fives. Such dynamics vary widely from place to place, and from person to person. I doubt that you can avoid the tension completely. In fact, I doubt that you should: there is much to learn from America's social reality, and much that you can contribute to improving it, even if only by connecting with people who are otherwise left aside.

NEGOTIATING CULTURE SHOCK

Every university with an international interest seems to offer advice on culture shock, though I have never found their advice useful. While writing this chapter, I looked at 20 university websites and found the same generic statement about difference causing difficulties, hardly evolved since Oberg's (1960) seminal definition. To help yourself, they say, just be aware that you'll go through a four-stage coping process ending in assimilation, rejection, or a cosmopolitan identity.

The problem with this advice is that we are neither tourists nor migrants, and we typically plan to be there for a substantial, albeit temporary, duration. We are seeking difference, and intending to learn at a deeply transformative level. Difference cannot be what shocks us if it's what we are there to enjoy. Having observed and helped both international and American students through culture shock, I have come to think that it is *unprepared* difference that matters. These differences are often so tiny and inconsequential that we don't expect them to matter in the slightest. They matter a great deal, though, when we aren't expecting them, and when we are tired from having enthusiastically engaged with difference all day.

My advice is to prepare retreats. When you have had a full day of intercultural novelty, skip the nearest coffee shop (which would involve still more intercultural engagement), and instead go somewhere that you know intimately well. It is not difference that you need a break from, but the risk of unpredictability.

Many students deal pre-emptively with culture shock by avoiding it. Sometimes this follows from the university or a student association having helpfully sent "people like you" to engineer a welcoming arrival, and you end up with an instant social circle that insulates you from the surrounding world. We worked hard to undo that unplanned insulation at my last American university because it undermined curricular goals concerned with community diversity (which includes all international students), mastering English, and collegiality. Those communities can offer comfort via familiarity, but don't feel obliged to hang out with them forever, nor to avoid associating with others elsewhere. Sticking exclusively with people like you almost guarantees missing out on some of the most worthwhile things that an American education offers.

LEARNING AND TEACHING THE AMERICAN WAY

The American graduate classroom can be alien for Americans and international students alike, but international students may experience a few extra complications. Accent occasionally complicated my classes. I had the advantage of having heard many Americans on television and radio, but my classmates hadn't heard many who spoke like me. Switching from British to American spelling took some time, with every conversion rule seeming flawed by exceptions. Over time I simply got used to the variations, and am now "bilingual" in English spelling. On the other hand, when it came time to teach, my accent enabled me to be much blunter about low performance and poor conduct without being interpreted as insulting. "Cultured," they called it. Several American colleagues openly wished for an accent like mine at times like that.

I was also tripped up by a few instances of assumed knowledge. Mentions of the "antebellum" and "interbellum" periods made conversations seem to jump irrationally between centuries until I found out that these terms refer to the War of Independence and the Civil War of the 18th and 19th centuries, core elements of

American identity, and not, as had always been the case for me, to the World Wars of the 20th century. The "War of 1812," likewise, turned out not to be the French invasion of Russia, but the Anglo-American war that began in the same year. I thought of "Jim Crow" as obscure military slang, but in America, it's an emotive term for institutionalized racism.

More recently, peer feedback and grading has become more widespread in American teaching. Regardless of whether American undergraduates like it, many have at least experienced it. For students coming from other academic cultures, however, peer grading may seem both novel and ridiculous—why cross the world to study with esteemed scholars, only to be subjected to the novice-level ignorance of students like yourself (McLeay & Wesson, 2014)? Explaining how and why peer grading is a good idea requires more space than I have here (Nichol, Thomson, & Breslin, 2014). Give it a chance, and see what you can re-apply to your own teaching later. Think of it as a form of collegiality, at the very least. You do stand to learn about the difficult art of giving useful feedback, and also from the kinds of feedback that your peers are equipped to give. Participating sincerely may also build your future professional network.

You could find that graduate coursework cramps your style, especially if you already have a dissertation in mind or have already started on it. Independent reading courses—one-on-one arrangements between you and a professor—can advance your intentions. Do not underestimate, though, the chance to broaden your knowledge. You get to do this because American graduate courses often assume very little background. I took the opportunity to gain a grounding in art history, which I had never studied before. I also took a graduate laboratory course in biomedical engineering out of sheer curiosity, and I was never disadvantaged relative to the biology majors, or even those pursuing doctorates in biomedical engineering. There were even introductory language courses designed for scholarly reading rather than the tourism-dogged introductions offered to undergraduates. In American coursework I found opportunities not available in the universities that I had come from.

FINDING A DISSERTATION ADVISOR

Every program has its own way of matching students with advisors, and you may well have come in with clear preferences from your application phase. Advice given to domestic students also applies here, though there is an extra question for international students: Which prospective advisors are good at supporting international students? Intercultural skills vary between individuals, and I know of no university that offers its faculty anything more than introductory guidance to working with international students.

Unfortunately, prejudice also plays into advisor assignment. I have dealt with students enduring what could be considered abusive advisors, and have heard many stories about how those advisors did their PhDs under an advisor at least as horrible, and now perpetuate the cycle of abuse. Be alert to such circumstances; you may be able to avoid or mollify them. Return to your reasons for choosing your program of study, and remember that, in spite of the bad things one hears, wonderful supervisors abound. In my experience, the good people are the majority.

TEACHING AMERICAN UNDERGRADUATES

Serving as a teaching assistant (TA, occasionally "teaching fellow") can be especially difficult for people educated abroad, simply because you will have no idea what happens in an undergraduate American classroom. Americans often have to recalibrate their expectations too, owing to the wide breadth of undergraduate experiences, but at least they have experienced some version of this themselves.

American universities perceive these problems too. Many hold workshops aimed at helping international students to better understand American undergraduate classroom culture, assessment standards, and interpersonal relations. There are also workshops on accent adjustment, responding to possible complaints about the "incomprehensible" foreign TA.

Your students could vary a great deal. You might also be confounded by students who argue with you in class, marshaling ideas from other disciplines. It is important to remember that your role is not to assert correctness, but to nurture their educations, and the kind of education you should nurture depends on the curriculum.

That said, cultural exchange goes both ways. Just as you have a lot to gain from learning how to teach in this academic culture, you also have a lot of value to bring from your own. I find it hard to imagine a good argument against elevating the students' aspirations whenever you think they could be higher. Every time I've tried it, the students have responded positively. Some have told me that they deeply yearn for teachers who hold them to the high intellectual goals that they, like you, live for.

Overall, think of teaching as part of your experiential education. You can build credentials simply by doing it, and keeping good records such as the number of students you teach, your teaching evaluations, formal observations of your teaching, and materials that you prepare for class. Through this experience you can build expertise in both the subject and in the craft of teaching itself. Those skills translate directly to speaking at conferences, defending your dissertation, and pitching ideas to venture capitalists and other potential supporters, including potential employers.

CONCLUSION

Above all, I agree with the emphasis that study advisors place on achieving a "good fit." What complicates the fitting process for international students is getting information that actually helps. Take your time to explore the vast swathes of information that inevitably result from investigating American graduate programs, getting to learn how the system—with its many variations—operates. Keep in mind why and how you want to pursue graduate education, and look for a program and institution with compatible resources and values. Think ahead to the breadth of careers that lie beyond graduation and how you can prepare for multiple opportunities—including the non-academic majority—while working on your dissertation. Think also about optimizing the cross-cultural exchange—both in general, and also in the academy. Make the most of your experience to embrace the academic culture, and to give back to that culture, so that both continue to grow.

REFERENCES

Golde, C. M. (1998). Beginning graduate school: Explaining first-year doctoral attrition. *New Directions for Higher Education, 101,* 55–64. doi: 10.1002/he.10105

Jackson, B. (2015). University rankings: How well do they measure service quality? *Portal: Libraries and the Academy, 15,* 315–330. doi: 10.1353/pla.2015.0026

Logan, J., & Curry, J. (2015). A liberal arts education: Global trends and challenges. *Christian Higher Education, 14,* 66–79. doi: 10.1080/15363759.2015.973344

McLeay, F., & Wesson, D. (2014). Chinese versus UK marketing students' perceptions of peer feedback and peer assessment. *International Journal of Management Education, 12,* 142–150. doi: 10.1016/j.ijme.2014.03.005

Nichol, D., Thomson, A., & Breslin, C. (2014). Rethinking feedback processes in higher education: A peer review perspective. *Assessment and Evaluation in Higher Education, 39,* 102–122. doi: 10.1080/02602938.2013.795518

Oberg, K. (1960). Cultural shock: Adjustments to new cultural environments. *Practical Anthropology, 7,* 177–182.

CHAPTER TWENTY

Southern Exposure

Learning Through Experiences Overseas

WILLIAM M. HURTES

INTRODUCTION

It was almost 15 years after completing my undergraduate studies before I decided to go back to school. In that time I worked for one of the largest humanitarian organizations in the world and was responsible for hiring more than my share of staff. Over the years, resume after resume came into my office for review, and frankly, after a while, they all started to look alike. The applicants that stood out had two things. They had a unique experience or outlook and they were able to relate that experience or outlook to the job. I found that their experiences instilled in them a sense of confidence and enabled them to better work with diverse people.

For many, graduate school is a way to gain experiences and broaden their outlook. For me, deciding to go back to school was a big step. Deciding *where* to go was equally as large. I found the two decisions, *why* and *where*, completely intertwined. Graduate school is largely about asking yourself difficult questions and critically analyzing them in a way that you may not have before. Understanding what you want will help guide the process of finding the right school, selecting the right advisors, defining your area of specialization, and meeting your expectations.

Part vignette, part discussion, this chapter uses memories of my own experiences to emphasize the benefits of leaving the country to pursue your graduate studies. You may realize, as I did, that there are many benefits to studying abroad.

This chapter will explore these benefits. It explores a range of intellectual, social, cultural, and interpersonal benefits that you just can't match in a domestic school experience. Studying abroad has enabled me to improve my ability to communicate with people, manage change, broaden my worldview, and set me apart from other job applicants. The United States has been built on a mix of cultures, and, with global trends, more and more employers are looking for staff who can relate to diverse audiences and who have international experience.

SOUTHERN EXPOSURE

I step off the ferry into the misty rain to find myself much farther South than I have ever been. Walking next to the beach, the sparsely paved roads, which are more like allies, eventually lead to my hotel for the weekend. The tattered building shows signs of the harsh winters and I find refuge from the rain and driving wind in the office. All the rooms look dark and no one seems to be around to check me in. A note greets me on the counter inviting me to take the key and let myself in. "We'll take care of checking you in tomorrow" it promises.

After collecting my things, I tentatively make my way down the hall and through the open dining room and kitchen to my room. It strikes me how different this is from home. The entire building appears to be unoccupied and unlocked all at the same time. Signs invite guests to make themselves at home by lighting a fire in the living room or curling up on one of the many overstuffed couches with a book from the library. There are no guards, no barred windows, no warning signs, no indication that this is an unsafe or unwelcoming place. It's nice. There is a sense of trust. A sense of respect between staff and guest. It is welcoming. And appealing!

I have been looking forward to a few days off. For the last several weeks, I have been conducting interviews and collecting data for my research while traveling all over the South Island of New Zealand. This is a good opportunity to relax for a few days and explore another part of this amazing country before starting back up again on Monday.

The next morning I find the most unexpected French crepery, which is a surprise as there are only two restaurants on the entire island, and strike up a conversation with the only other customer, Destiny. She tells me about growing up in the States, going to school in France, and how she ending up living on a small island in the Pacific at the bottom of the world. She tells how hard it was initially moving to a new country, not understanding the culture, customs, traditions, and language. "There is only so much that you can learn in a French class. You have to live it!" she says.

Destiny says that she learned the hard way how important understanding someone's culture is. She starts by saying that her mother loved carnations, so for every special occasion, there were always flowers around the house. She says that when she was invited to a fancy dinner at a neighbor's house she wanted to bring a gift. "I brought fresh flowers for my host, but I never realized what a bad idea that was." She recognizes the perplexed look on my face and goes on to say that a friend later told her that the carnations she brought were a sign of bad luck. Her friend also said that in France, any gift of flowers should have been sent after the day of the party as a thank you, not something to be arranged and displayed at the time.

It strikes me how little I know about the etiquette of gift-giving in France or any other part of the world. I remember back to living in a small mountain community in Costa Rica. The town only had about 10,000 residents, but when 200 graduate students moved in from Korea, Nepal, Kenya, Hungary, Argentina, and 57 other countries, it transformed into a multicultural mecca. It also transformed my understanding. I was confronted with a lot of people who grew up with different experiences than me, different customs, and different perspectives on virtually everything. This was not just one or two people who I could easily dismiss. This was a complete and total immersion in change.

I saw an article several years later where the author talked about how your world becomes a whole lot bigger after living abroad. I remember one night in particular where a group of us went to dinner at the most amazing Lebanese restaurant in San Jose. It may sound strange going for Lebanese food in Central America, but that is not half as strange as what actually happened that evening. We sat down and proceeded with the typical small talk and toasting, but that did not last long. Conversation quickly turned to the demonstrations occurring in Egypt at that time. We all had a very different understanding of what was happening and why. Maricelly from Puerto Rico, Marion from France, Leticia from Brazil, Wiktor from Poland, Carly from Canada, and I continued to raise points about poverty, police corruption, unemployment, democracy, the use of military forces, and the pros and cons of civil disobedience. After several hours of intense discussions we commented on the way home how listening to our friends' perspectives had changed our own thoughts about the issue.

This was not a singular occurrence among random expatriates. The more we discussed complex issues, listened to other perspectives, and allowed ourselves to be open to new ideas, the more we learned about our own perspectives, beliefs, and expectations. I never had conversations like this in the States. This is what we were in Costa Rica to do, to learn. We were all there studying for a graduate degree, and found that by getting different groups together, we learned more and it ended up bringing us closer together.

Destiny nods in agreement as she recalls similar experiences in her travels. She says that she has met some of her best friends while working with a human trafficking campaign in Asia, as well as some of the most despicable. One thing her experiences taught her was how to negotiate with people she did not trust or agree with. She attributes the success her group had in freeing young women from slavery to their ability to work with people with different beliefs.

"Wow, for you travel was more than an adventure. You were able to use your cultural experiences to save lives," I tell her. At this point I have nothing but admiration for her, and nothing more to say. As we finish the last sip of coffee we thank each other for sharing and I wander out the door for a hike.

Making my way up the hills and through native gardens I cannot help but think back on how living in so many different places with so many different cultures has changed my own life. Growing up in the "Bible Belt" I believe that I had a carefully crafted worldview and perception of historical, social, and political issues. All of which was based on the status of where I lived and who I lived with. All my friends looked like me, lived like me, and largely valued the same things that I did. Life was easy and there was little that challenged my worldview. Well, that was until I moved to Utah.

Local wisdom says that there are really only two reasons that people move to Utah. For some it is to be at the center of the Church of Jesus Christ of Latter-day Saints, headquartered in Salt Lake City, and for others it is to be at the center of adventure sports. Whatever the reason, religion is ingrained in almost every part of daily life and culture there. Not having any exposure to the LDS Church, I had a lot to learn and adjust to. My views on baptism, marriage, spirits, the idea of what a church is, and even family and service to the community were blown away and expanded at the same time. I worked closely with leaders from the LDS Church and other social service organizations over the 10 years I spent there. During that time I was so impressed with the commitment to service that members of the LDS faith repeatedly demonstrated.

After hundreds of Hurricane Katrina evacuees landed in Salt Lake City, they were housed at a military base for the first few weeks. Watching their faces when they arrived in Utah, it was clear that they were not told where they were going or what to expect when they got there. Needless to say, the evacuees were overwhelmed. Overwhelmed by what they had just been through and overwhelmed by the unfamiliar sights, sounds, smells, and customs of Utah. During their time at the military base, I saw groups feeding and clothing the evacuees, providing medical services, and offering spiritual counseling. On one of the first days, a colleague and church leader recognized that many of the evacuees were asking for cigarettes. Putting his personal and religious beliefs aside, he purchased a carton and distributed cigarettes to anyone who needed them. He said that a crisis like this is hard enough without the added burden of withdrawal. His actions removed a complication and enabled them to recovery more quickly. He later said that it was the humane thing to do.

As I sit on the side of this mountain overlooking the sandy bay below, I realize that sometimes it takes extraordinary events to enable us to view things in a new way. Sometimes it takes extraordinary events to allow us to recognize the importance of someone's habits, or customs, or culture, even if they are in contradiction with our own.

On the hike back to my room, I must have been lost in my own thoughts as I nearly step in front of a speeding car. In one of those images that flashed before my eyes, I see myself reading a book on the balcony overlooking a street. Below there are five or six kids no older than 8 playing soccer. It is an intense game that is occasionally interrupted by passing cars. My mother's voice echoes in my head, and I almost shout out, "It's too dangerous to be out playing in the street!"

The view is from my apartment in Costa Rica. Day after day, month after month, these kids play and play as I watch. Never seeing any parents hanging around, I begin to realize how independent and smart these young kids are. First, I respect the fact that they are outside, playing with other children, and getting some exercise. They are young and savvy. They develop their own signals to warn each other about oncoming cars, they change the rules of the game to accommodate the constant interruptions, and they encourage all the neighbors to play, regardless of how bad they are. This seems so different from what I remember as a child. These kids learn from an early age to get along and they learn how to adapt in the face of adversity. Nothing is going to prevent them from having a good time.

Adaptation is something that I was becoming more and more familiar with. Life in the United States seemed easy, but living and going to school in Central America was all about adaptation. The language, food, etiquette, customs, and culture were all unfamiliar. Every time something new, or different, or scary, popped up, I thought about those children outside my apartment. Since finishing my undergraduate degree, every job or challenge I was faced with required me to adapt to a new situation and develop unique solutions. I had been doing so for so long that I developed a confidence in it, until those kids opened my eyes. They taught me a lot about persistence and overcoming challenges. I use their lessons today as I work with difficult people on complex projects. I seem to remember Michelle Obama saying something similar about study abroad programs making you "more marketable in the U. S."

It is a welcome sight, when I get back from my hike, to find that a few more people checked in. One is an American who came to New Zealand to study midwifery and her sister who is visiting. After a few bottles of wine and a frustratingly large jigsaw puzzle, I have to know why someone would travel all the way from Seattle, Washington, to train as a midwife. Sara says that New Zealand has one of the best training programs in the world and she wanted to learn from the best. This makes a lot of sense to me. She knew what she wanted to study and knew where to get the education and experience to be successful. Specifically, she wants to work in rural areas, and while we were talking, she gets her work-study assignment. She is heading out to a small group of islands in the middle of the Pacific, a 4-hour flight from any major hospital. Now that's rural!

I cannot help but relate with Sara's reasoning. I had left the United States several years earlier to study. By far the most common question I get is, why? In a time when so many people from around the world come to the United States for an education, why would I leave? Because I have been asked this so many times, I have had time to really think about this. It boils down to one thing. I wanted a different perspective.

Over time four criteria emerged that guided my search. First, I wanted a university and department that was accredited and internationally respected, much like Sara. Knowing that I may come back to the United States to work, it was critical that my degree be recognized by future employers. Second, and this may sound obvious for students in fields such as mathematics, or business, or the physical sciences, I wanted a university that had a research center dedicated to my studies (the somewhat obscure field of disaster risk reduction). I looked at hundreds and hundreds of degree programs but there were only a few dozen that had internationally recognized research centers. Because I had a very clear understanding of my research interest, it was critically important that I find a supervising advisor with the right combination of knowledge, experience, and disposition. As I had seen several student-advisor relationships last longer than some marriages. I knew that this had to be someone whom I could relate to, work with, and respect. The final consideration was that the university had to be in a place that I would enjoy living in. So much of my memories and learning from Costa Rica were from the people and culture, that I was not willing to sacrifice four years of my life just for a degree. The area had to offer something new that would both challenge my current perspective and be pleasant. Hell, I could get a degree anywhere, so if I was going to do something a little different it had to benefit me in multiple ways.

Seeing the sun come up the next morning is a welcome change to the last several days of rainy and cold weather. Sara, her sister, Amanda, and I set out for another hike around the island. Walking down the old logging road we talk about the places we've traveled, the experiences we've had, and the people we have known. Amanda says that when she landed in Athens, Greece, for a high school study-abroad program, how relieved she was to be met at the airport by her host family. "They were so welcoming and showed me all around the place and made me feel at home," she says. Even though it has been many years since, she still keeps in touch with the family and saw them when they visited Seattle a few years ago.

That night over dinner and a few more bottles of wine, a few others join in on the conversation. Jamie, a New Zealand university student, says, "Ya, me and all my mates took an OE after high school." "What in the world is an OE?" asks Amanda, and Jamie explains that most Kiwis save up for years to take an "Oversees Experience." Jamie says "It's part of being Kiwi. An OE is part of our language. It's part of what we do." Everyone I meet in New Zealand has taken an OE and talks about what a great experience it was meeting people from all over the world and building relationships.

On a recent trip to see the family in South Carolina, I had the chance to catch up with a high school friend. We talked for hours about politics, data mining, corporate farming, homeland security, and, well, anything else that was on our minds. We disagreed on almost every point. Leaving the bar that night, I realized how much my experience had changed me. I did a little digging the next day and discovered that most of my high school classmates still live in the same town with many of our friends. I wanted something different. A different perspective on the world. Many Kiwis get this as part of their OE.

As I pack up my things the next morning, I happen to run into Sara who says that she just got an e-mail from a friend in Trinidad who asked if she knew anything about a particular project taking place in Mozambique. While she did not, she was able to connect her with a friend, originally from Brazil, whom she had studied with several years before, who was working on that very project. It is funny that we were just talking the night before about how traveling builds networks.

My own networks have expanded from not only the students I have studies with but also the professors and locals. Over the last several years I have reached out to many of them for help on projects or for a different perspective on issues. I have worked and volunteered in the places that I've lived, which has given me an entirely new view of work practices, ethics, laws, and benefits of service. These experiences have lead to a more culturally sensitive global view. It has also provided for a more diverse and well-rounded list of references.

I sit on the ferry that morning; the conversations over the last few days keep ringing in my head. I think about how lucky I was to spend time in some of the most beautiful places in the world, with some of the most amazing people. I think about how the welcome note that greeted me at the beginning of this island stay was so indicative of the New Zealand culture. I don't know that I have ever felt so welcomed by so many different people. The fact that doors are seldom locked leads you to understand what a safe and respectful place this is. It strikes me that every time I ride the public bus, everyone, even the teenagers, thank the bus driver as they exit.

A buzz on the ferry brings me back to the present. Passengers are rushing to the windows to see penguins perched on a nearby rock. As I try to shake off the excitement, I realize that I'm sure not in Utah any more. I realize that I would not have met Destiny and heard how her experiences of travel and working with different cultures had led to the freeing of those young girls. I realize how much I had to learn about adaptability from the children playing soccer in the street. I realize how a casual conversation over a meal of Baba Ghanouj and Kibbeh Nayyeh in Central America could open my eyes to so many different perspectives. I realize how important Sara's, and Jamie, and even my own, network of friends is.

I get a cup of tea and sit back on a bench to stare out the window at the Foveaux Strait. I realize that the relationships I have built and the experiences I have had make me who I am today. I realize that I would not trade studying abroad for anything.

Contributors

Harry C. Boyte Senior Scholar in Public Work Philosophy at the Center for Democracy and Citizenship at Augsburg College and a senior fellow at the University of Minnesota's Humphrey School of Public Affairs, is the author and co-author of eight books including *Everyday Politics, The Citizen Solution, and The Wingspread Declaration on Renewing the Civic Mission of Research Universities* with Elizabeth Hollander. In 2012 Boyte coordinated the American Commonwealth partnership, a coalition invited by the White House Office of Public Engagement to strengthen higher education as a public good

Melissa Dennihy (PhD) is assistant professor of English at Queensborough Community College, City University of New York, where her research focuses on multi-ethnic U.S. literatures and the teaching of writing and literature. She earned her PhD in English from The Graduate Center, City University of New York.

Jaime Guzmán is currently attending the University of Denver getting a doctorate degree in Communication Studies with an emphasis on critical intercultural communication. He received his MA in Communication Studies from California State University, Los Angeles, with an emphasis in rhetoric.

Yessica Garcia Hernandez is a doctoral student at the University of California, San Diego, in the Department of Ethnic Studies. She obtained her MA in Chicana/o Studies from California State University, Los Angeles, and her bachelor's from the University of California, Riverside. Using an ethnographic approach, she studies the culture of Latino immigrants in the United States. She is currently working on a documentary about Banda music and the fans of Chicana singer Jenni Rivera.

Alison Hicks is a PhD student in the School of Information Studies at Charles Sturt University, Australia, and the Romance Language librarian at the University of Colorado, Boulder, USA. With an MA from the University of St Andrews, Scotland, and an MSIS from the University of Texas, Austin, USA, Alison's research centres on information literacy, and the nature of these practices within intercultural transitions.

Tabatha Hoffmeyer is a Special Education teacher who holds an MAT with an emphasis on Mild to Moderate Disabilities from Webster University. She is currently taking coursework to gain certification in the areas of severe disabilities and behavior analysis. Tabatha also serves on the board of a state-wide organization that promotes advocacy and awareness for individuals on the autism spectrum.

Christopher A. Huff (PhD) is an assistant professor of history at Beacon College in Leesburg, Florida. He received his doctorate at the University of Georgia in 2012, where he completed a dissertation that explored the New Left and counterculture in Atlanta during the late 1960s and early 1970s. At Beacon he teaches a variety of courses in United States and world history and has published several articles on Southern student movements from the Sixties era.

William M. Hurtes is an educator with 20 years of experience developing and delivering courses using experiential techniques. Largely focusing on health, safety, and disaster topics, he has worked with a wide range of youth organizations, universities, government offices, and non-profits. His background as a wilderness guide and disaster manager combined with his experiences living, working, and studying in the United States, Costa Rica, and New Zealand greatly influence his perspectives on learning, understanding, and meaning.

Atsushi Iida (PhD) is an assistant professor of English in the University Education Center at Gunma University, Japan. He was awarded his PhD in English (Composition and TESOL) at Indiana University of Pennsylvania, PA. His research interests include second language writing, literature in second language education, and writing for academic publication. He has published his work in various journals including *Scientific Study of Literature, English Teaching Forum, Asian EFL Journal,* and *Assessing Writing.*

Alistair Kwan (PhD) is a lecturer (assistant professor) in the University of Auckland's Centre for Learning and Research in Higher Education. He studied at

Auckland, Melbourne, and Yale. He then worked at Yale and Rochester for several years, became a U.S. permanent resident, and thinks of the Northeast as home. He teaches faculty to improve their teaching, runs a future faculty program, and researches historical and current student learning processes.

Ju Seong Lee is a doctoral student at the University of Illinois at Urbana-Champaign. His research interests include World Englishes, technology-integrated learning in second-/foreign-language classroom (via videoconference, tele-collaboration, wearable devices), and issues of international students.

Magdalena Leszko (PhD) is a psychologist and a Fulbright scholar from Poland. She graduated from the University of Kansas and is currently a post-doctoral fellow at Northwestern University in Chicago. During her time at graduate school, Dr. Leszko successfully applied for a variety of travel and research scholarships. She received the Fulbright scholarship to study in the United States, and recently participated in the Millennial Train Project, which enabled her to travel across the United States and conduct research on dementia prevention.

Alison S. Marzocchi (PhD) is an assistant professor in the Mathematics Department at California State University in Fullerton, California. She is a 2015 graduate of the Mathematics Education PhD program at the University of Delaware. Her dissertation is titled *Investigating Changes of Underrepresented Students' Mathematics Identities into Their First Year of College*. Broadly, her research is motivated by improving the recruitment and retention of underrepresented students in postsecondary mathematics. Before pursing her doctoral degree, Alison was a volleyball coach and a high school teacher of mathematics and computer science.

Christopher McMaster (PhD) is assistant professor of education at Augsburg College, Minneapolis. He has pursued graduate study in the United States (special education), UK (MA and PGCE/teaching), and New Zealand (where he earned a doctorate in Education). He has contributed to and co-edited editions of *Surviving and Succeeding* in each of these locations.

Caterina Murphy (PhD) is a passionate educationalist, currently freelancing her academic leadership services through *AcademicExpressNZ* to tertiary institutions, individuals, schools, and businesses. Mentoring and lifting the aspirations of others is her passion. She has a Master of Education (Hons) from Massey University and a PhD (Indigenous Studies) from Te Whare Wānanga o Awanuiārangi. Her professional and research interests include career counselling, early years education, teaching practice, mentoring, qualitative research, gifted education, and oral history methodology. This is her fourth edited book.

Ken Nielsen (PhD) is a senior lecturer and associate director for the Writing Center at NYU Abu Dhabi. He graduated from the Theater Program at the Graduate Center, City University of New York. His work concerns theatre history, cultural studies, and composition. Both his research and his teaching of composition are invested in furthering an understanding of the interplay of popular culture, identity, cultural differences, rhetorics, and lived experience.

B. J. Parker is a graduate student in the Religion Department at Baylor University. His research includes the theology of suffering in the Book of Psalms as well as the convergence of visual art and research. He has published on both the Psalter and using art as a means of research. When not writing papers, B. J. enjoys drawing, painting, and woodworking.

Lara Rose Roberts is seeking her master's degree in English Literature while getting distracted by the foothills of the Rocky Mountains at Colorado State University, Fort Collins. Fitting for someone with her disordered brain functioning, her interests are split between a love of the indoors (literature) and a love of the outdoors (mountains). Her thesis will try to mash those interests together in the way that a study of literature can involve studying how humans have historically viewed their place on this planet.

Danielle Shepherd is a PhD student in the Exercise Physiology Program under Biomedical Sciences at West Virginia University. Her research interests are centered on studying how the heart functions during diabetes mellitus and particularly, how this disease affects the mitochondria. After obtaining her PhD, her goal is to pursue a career in scientific education and outreach, where she will work with and excite young students about science through a hands-on educational approach.

Debra Trusty (MA) is a PhD candidate at Florida State University working toward a degree in Classical Archaeology. She has participated in archaeological projects in Greece since 2006. Her dissertation focuses on ceramic cooking vessels from Late Bronze Age Greece and the evidence they provide on the political economy of the Mycenaean world. She received a National Science Foundation grant in 2010 to conduct her research, which includes microscopic and chemical analyses on these vessels.

Raisa Alvarado Uchima is a Culture and Communication Studies doctoral student at the University of Denver. She completed her MA in Communication Studies at California State University, Long Beach, with an emphasis in rhetoric and performance studies. Her academic areas of focus are in critical intercultural communication and Chicana feminism.

Timothy Weldon is a PhD candidate in Anthropology at Rutgers University. He holds an MA in Economic and Social History from the University of Manchester, and a BA in Sociology and Anthropology from West Virginia University. His research focuses on alternative understandings of democracy, grassroots and lived political experiences, squatting, and leftist autonomous movements, primarily in Europe and the United States. Tim also serves on the editorial board of *Social Movements and Change*.

Nicholas R. Werse is a graduate of George W. Truett Theological Seminary and is currently pursuing his PhD in Hebrew Bible at Baylor University. He is published in the fields of biblical studies and church history, and focuses his present research agenda on Hebrew prophetic literature. His contribution to the present volume emerges from his participation with the Baylor University Conyers Scholars Program, as well as countless conversations with his colleagues in the graduate student lounge.

Rebecca Zimmer is a doctoral candidate in History at the University of Southern Mississippi, where she is also a graduate assistant. During the 2009–2010 academic year, she was an adjunct lecturer at the University of North Carolina, Pembroke. Her dissertation is tentatively entitled, *Temperance and Woman Suffrage: Success and Struggle in Mississippi at the Turn of the Twentieth Century*, and considers the relationship between the Woman's Christian Temperance Union and the woman suffrage movement in Mississippi.